GROWING UP IN ALCOHOLISM, VIOLENCE & DYSFUNCTION

Listening To My Inner Child

MICHAEL WILLIAMS

THANK YOU FOR YOUR INVESTMENT IN THIS BOOK. YOU CAN LOCATE OTHER BOOKS BY THIS AUTHOR AT WWW.AMAZON.COM OR FOLLOW THIS AUTHOR FOR NEW EDITIONS, NEW BOOKS, SPEAKING ENGAGEMENTS AND SPECIAL EVENTS.

IT IS MY FONDEST HOPE THIS WORK WILL HELP YOU WITH YOUR PAIN!

ALSO BY MICHAEL WILLIAMS

THE WORKBOOK FOR GROWING UP IN ALCOHOLISM, VIOLENCE & DYSFUNCTION
Wakening & Listening to My Inner Child
Dysfunctional Child Publishing, 2016

INSPIRATIONAL STORIES OF THE HOMELESS
Dignity, Nobility, Decency
Dysfunctional Child Publishing, 2016

Currently Available on Amazon.com
Paperback or Kindle

Legal Notice & Disclaimer

Nothing contained in this book is to be considered medical, therapeutic, legal, or tax advice for your specific situation. Any diet and nutrition information in this book has not been evaluated by the FDA and is not intended to treat, diagnose, cure, or prevent any disease. This information is not intended as a substitute for the advice or medical care of your own physicians, attorneys, therapists or tax advisors and you should consult with their own physicians, therapists, attorneys, or tax advisors prior to taking any personal action with respect to the information contained in this book. This book and all of its contents are intended for educational, entertainment and informational purposes only. The information in this book is believed to be reliable, but is presented without guaranty or warranty.

By reading further, you agree to release the author and publisher from any damages or injury associated with your use of the material in this book. Some products mentioned in this book are under trademark or service mark protection. Product and service names and terms are used only in an editorial fashion for educational purposes with no intent to infringe or dilute such trademarks. If reference is provided to specific products, those references are for illustration purposes only and no warranty for such products or fitness for a particular purpose is implied. Such references may be to affiliates that compensate the publisher or author if a purchase is made through the author, publisher, or book's referral. Such products are available at a wide variety of retailers and no recommendation is made or implied to use any particular retailer.

Published by

Dysfunctional Child Publishing
williamsmike4171930@gmail.com
Escondido, California

Second Printing 2016
Printed in the United States of America

ISBN: 10: 0692709851
ISBN- 13: 978-0692709856

DEDICATION

This book is dedicated to my childhood friends, who never questioned childhood because they died within.

Alvin Jefferies
Billy Bateman
Claude Green
Stanley Brown
Theodore Richwood

In death, you bequeathed me the gift of perspective for the creation of life.

Thank you!

ACKNOWLEDGMENTS

I give thanks to the master of creation.

I thank my siblings, parents, uncles, Bill Gibbons,
Donna Harrell, Dr. G. Christine Taylor, Theresa Evans, Susan
Christie & Delya Rahmani.

I thank my first family of choice David, Betty, Pamela, Dan, Rebecca,
Roland, Marilyn, Richard, Patti and Andy.

I gratefully acknowledge the support of Dr. J. Keith Auerbach,
Novella Harrison, Charles Massey, L.C.S.W., M. Div.,
& Dr. Maya J. Klein

Preface

There were huge holes in my memories of childhood.

I was living the life I had learned to live as a child growing up in alcoholism, violence and dysfunction. How could I do anything else? It was all I knew!

I do not comprehend how excruciation becomes throbbing, aching and agonizing but it does; and that is somehow an improvement. It was so painful for so long it was no longer recognizable as pain, it was my normal.

That is the saddest moment of childhood for those of us who grew up in alcoholism, violence and dysfunction. I still feel that moment. I still feel the moment I accepted distress, anguish and sorrow as normal. I was ten years old and it happened on an interior staircase. In that moment my childhood heart was in too many pieces to be recognized as a heart anymore. Upsetting, laborious, harrowing had become daily, routine, expected.

This is the moment the soul becomes separated from the inner child. The separation is not an act of abandonment it is an act of survival, waiting, hoping and praying for a more supportive/nurturing environment from which to exist.

I could not connect with others, like other people. I was not like other people. There was a part of me beyond my own reach; that bothered me. Peace was beyond any of my life-time state of affairs. My soul was tired far beyond my years. I was in denial of my most powerful reality, "pain."

Journaling assisted me. It was one of my first forms of learning how to care for myself in a healthy way just for the sake of myself. I decided to type my journal and realized I had sixty-eight typed pages. In that moment I knew I would finish the story. I did not know it would take a decade.

I have come to believe it was worth it. I was in the process of gathering and assembling those pieces of myself that had been abandoned and/or lost a long time ago. I was picking up, and retrieving pieces of myself. It is one of those jobs no one can ever do for us. I have to do it for myself.

It was the beginning of realizing that I had an inner voice. More so it was the initiation of listening to my inner voice. It was practicing the discipline of paying attention to myself in a meaningful and purposeful way. Some call it listening to the inner child lately I prefer to call it paying attention.

In childhood I was attempting to survive alcoholism, violence and dysfunction and that endeavor left scant energy for any emotional, mental or spiritual development which may be the function of childhood. I was otherwise busy trying to survive and/or save my own ass.

This is the story my inner child needed to tell, more importantly, it is the story my soul needed to hear for me to heal.

CONTENTS

ADOLESCENCE

COMING TO PEACE WITH CHILDHOOD

CHAPTER 1

FIRST MEMORIES

My first memory at the tender age of twenty-three months was of anger, fear, confusion, and resentment.

We walked up the stairs into the wood-framed shotgun house as my grandmother waited to receive us. As I struggled with the huge steps, scurrying to keep up, I did not know what was in the blanket that my father cradled to his breast. I did know that whatever it was, I did not like it. That is how my baby brother, whom I would come to love, entered my life.

It is my suspicion that prior to that moment, I had no memories because I had no worries; all of what I needed was supplied in abundance, therefore the function of memory served no purpose. Every memory would have been identical - an accumulation of memories of abundance of everything, love, milk, food, and nurturing.

I gave birth to memory as a tool. For the first time in my life threats now existed. I now know I was feeling vulnerable, however my twenty-three-month-old mind could not comprehend such. I could only perceive a threat to love and abundance. I gave birth to memory as my heart conceived suspicion, fear, and resentment. That original fear that the abundance of love may not be abundance after all has never left me. It has permeated my every word, thought, action, and deed from that moment until this day.

My grandmother always held a special place in my life, not because she was my grandmother, not because of what she did for me, but because of the way she made me feel.

Times spent with grandma were exuberant and joyful. Out of all the people I have met in my life, my grandmother is the only one who I am sure cherished me. In her eyes I could do no wrong.

In her eyes, I was perfect as I was. In her eyes, I was loved, cherished, and nurtured.

I have never enjoyed doing chores. All throughout childhood until today, I avoided or put off doing chores. With grandma, things were different. I used to love drying dishes as she washed. I think I loved the way she stared into my eyes, the gaze and total amazement that she felt at the fact that I existed. I loved doing chores with grandma not because I loved doing the chores, but because I loved being with her and the sense that we were doing something together.

In retrospect, I was not a good dish-dryer. I can remember leaving dishes wet from time to time, but with her it did not make a difference. With her the dishes were O.K. because I was O.K., with her it was simply O.K. As time went on, I wanted to do more and more with her, wash clothes, fold clothes, put clothes on the line, and each time my inadequacy or ineptness was quite all right. I think that I may have loved my grandma more than I have loved anyone before or since.

It was while living in my grandma's house that I first discovered magic. Her house sat adjacent to a vacant lot - a childhood field of dreams and dream in it I did. The grass grew over four feet tall, or so it seemed; regardless it was over my head. In that field I killed my first lion, faced my first dragon, rescued my sister from the heathens, explored my first jungle, went to war with my baby brother, built my first treehouse and explored the farthest reaches of the universe.

It was while living in my grandma's house that I saw my first rainbow - red, yellow, green - and first made plans to go on an expedition to bring back the pot of gold at the end of the rainbow while wondering just how many soda pops, ice cream sundaes and candy bars a pot of gold would actually buy.

While living in my grandmother's house I first discovered the world of make-believe the world of magic, and the land of enchantment. I, my sister, and my brother would visit this land often, sometimes on a nightly basis. The three of us would wait for the nightly "good night" the bed-time kiss, and the lights to go out. Soon the circus would begin, with the three of us jumping up and down and up and down and up and down on the huge circus trampoline which was my sister's bed; we were the main performers in the center ring of our three-ring circus.

Then there were the trapeze artists. Once again we were the stars. We jumped from my top bunk bed onto my sister's bed right next to it in an amazing terror defying feat. Each night we would visit this circus until one day my baby sister, while in the midst of a triple somersault done backward without a net, landed on my baby brother below. Unfortunately, this near-death experience for my baby brother revealed itself in the form of a black eye forcing my parents to cease the circus. But we would continue to tell many stories of our circus after the lights were out, even if we did have to cut out the acrobatics.

It was in my grandmother's house that I first discovered Santa Claus, the Easter bunny and the tooth fairy, all of whom I might mention absolutely adored me and were rather fond of my sister and brother. I, my mother, brother, and sister had walked home from my mother's best friend's house. It was a warm April night, one which I really enjoyed. I walked up the stairs into the living room through the dining room and saw grandma stretched out on the kitchen floor. I cried out, "grandma, grandma, grandma" - no answer. I ran like the wind outside to summon my mama's help. "Mama, mama," she cried as the pain ran through my heart. Onto the phone, calling the ambulance, and to me what seemed like some type pow-wow among the adults who were already there.

What I remember most about my grandmother's death was listening to the adults around me, all of whom really scared me, and I remember kneeling in the kitchen doorway. I knelt in the doorway over my grandma right next to the kitchen sink where I had dried dishes as she had washed hundreds of times. Where she had stared into my eyes with that look of love hundreds of times, where she had whispered into my ears that she loved me hundreds of times and I knelt close to grandma and I blew air into her face. It was all that I knew how to do.

I had heard one of the adult's mention that she was not breathing, so I knelt there blowing air into her face and praying, "Grandma, please breath, grandma, please breath."

Looking back on that night, I realize that as I prayed I did not pray to God. I prayed to grandma, "grandma please breath, grandma please breath," but grandma never did breath for me no matter how hard I prayed. That was the first time, the last time, and the only time that grandma ever let me down.

As my grandmother lay there in a spit puddle around her face I knelt, I cried, I rocked, and I prayed, and I blew air into her face as she ascended to heaven. I wanted to hold her. I rubbed her forearm as she had so often rubbed mine, but I was scared. In the entire episode of my grandmother's death the only thing that I regret is that I did not hold her hug her to my breast for one last time as she had so often done with me.

The adults around us soon hustled me, my sister, and my brother upstairs. They fed us pumpkin pie and I vomited. Still over three decades later whenever I see pumpkin pie I still feel the urge to vomit.

I never saw my grandma again in that house. I saw her at the wake, at the funeral, and I know that she was at the cemetery, but it would never be the same again. I regret that I did not have an opportunity to say good-bye. I would have liked to have said good-bye to grandma, to tell her I missed her that I loved her, and that no one had ever made me feel the way that she did. Until this day when I am worried, troubled, or depressed I can always feel better by looking at myself through my grandmother's eyes.

I remember the women from my grandmother's social club telling me that I had to be the man of the house now. That nobody knew where my daddy was and that I had to be strong. They suspected that he was somewhere in Harlem, but no one knew for sure. I thought about going to Harlem to look for him, but I really wanted to play with my train set I had received the Christmas before.

My father showed up about two days before the funeral. He had taken five hundred dollars from grandma and disappeared before her death and had been gone several months. They accused him of murdering my grandma. They said that she had loved him and that she had died of a broken heart at the shock that he would steal from her.

Until this day I am unsure if my daddy's return was a good thing or a bad thing. My memories of his disappearance would be the first of a series of longings of a child for his father. I was happy to see my daddy again. I had missed him and longed for him. I loved looking at my father, staring into his eyes and observing him when he did not know I was looking.

In my seven years of life my grandma's death was my first experience of terror. Being told that my daddy had killed my grandma was my second experience of terror. Being told that I was going to have to be the man of the house was my third experience of terror. Wondering if my daddy would kill me the same way he had killed my grandma was the ultimate terror. As I reminisce about my grandmother's death I guess it was a terrorizing experience.

As we left the cemetery I can still hear my mama's screams "No, no, I can't leave my mama in that cold, hard ground." I turned around in that huge car and I stared at my grandma's grave surrounded with flowers. I watched the rain and snow coming down onto my grandmother's grave, and I worried who would cover up grandma and wouldn't she get cold in the ground and wet from the rain and snow.

That picture of my grandmother's grave in the rain and snow as we drove farther and farther away became permanently imbedded in my mind. I continue to recall that image even now. Although I did not realize it at the time, I believe that for the first time in my life I was experiencing the feeling of my heart breaking. I was losing a part of myself and feeling it die in the process.

I cried myself to sleep that night feeling very guilty that I could not find my way back to the cemetery to bring grandma a blanket. I worried and worried that grandma would be cold. Then I fell asleep. For what feels like forever and a day, I continued to wake up in the middle of the night thinking that I saw grandma standing in the doorway staring at me. I would wait for her to come home from work. I would try to eat dinner and wonder, "Where's grandma." Somehow I was unable to put together the Sunday cemetery visits with the fact that grandma did not come back.

I suspect the adults in my life lied to me during that time. I think my grandma was staring at me from that doorway. I think she missed me as much as I missed her and I think she wanted to say good-bye. Good-bye, grandma!

CHAPTER 2

BEST CHRISTMAS?

Grandma would continue to play an important part in my life for a long time to come. I associate grandma with wonder, with magic, with enchantment, and all that is good.

I would sit on the back porch of our home and watch my mother hang clothes on the line and my heart would ache for grandma. I helped my mother water the potted plants on that porch for months after my grandma's death. The plants grandma had so tenderly cared for were dying. Each time a plant would die I would hurt.

It was on my grandma's street I learned to ride a two-wheel bike, jump rope with my sister, use a hula hoop and a yo-yo. As time went on I continued to heal over my grandma's death but it would never be like it was again.

Winters in New Jersey are a special time for a child. There was always an anxious anticipation of the first snow. How deep would it be? How long would it snow? Would school close? Would it be the wet gooey stuff, which was great for making a snowman? Would it be the fluffy dry stuff, which was only good for throwing one's sister or brother into on their backsides?

I remember one snow was so deep that when we opened the front door there stood a wall of snow. It was great! I wanted to run straight into it as hard as I could. Parents being as parents are could not understand me and my siblings' excitement and exhilaration with this wonderful event.

I remember my daddy climbing out one of the windows and digging a way to the front door so we could get out of the house. When they finally let us out it was wonderful. Snow as far as the eye could see. All traffic was stopped and all the men on the street were trying to clean snow from the houses and the street so that traffic might once again flow. One of the great things about snow in New Jersey is that when it snows it may hang around for weeks on end. We built snowmen, snow houses, snow castles, snow caves, snow tunnels, and had snowball fights.

Some of my favorite times of childhood were in Weequahic Park in snow up to my knees wrestling with my sister and brother. I can still see my little sister and little brother in their bulky snow suits struggling to keep up with their older brother. We would spend a lot of time in that park as the years went on. I learned to love baseball in that park watching the neighborhood teams sponsored by different taverns compete. I especially always enjoyed watching my cousin Henry, "Bull" as he was so affectionately known.

I learned to fish in that park and I watched my first horse races in that park. More importantly, I learned to watch my father in that park. I learned there was something about manhood, a mystique, a brotherhood, something which I longed to grow into yet had not entered. On Fridays in the evenings often my daddy would simply drive through the park and I would watch him drive, run my hands through the curly kinks on the back of his head, watch the muscles in his forearms change as he drove, and watched the way he interacted with my mother. I was a child watching, ever watching, and attempting to discover that which I should become. In a way I often suspect that childhood is in essence a search for that which I should become - a curiosity about everything, optimism about each thing, and an imagination that was limitless in its creativity.

While on expedition with my siblings and other neighborhood children through the vacant lot next door to my grandmother's house we explored deepest, darkest Africa. I was the scout combination Tarzan for the expedition as I climbed a tree for a better view. This tree, which stood adjacent to my grandma's two-car garage, led me to the next childhood mystery - dancing and jumping on a roof, thereby plummeting through the decayed roof onto the concrete floor beneath. I sustained no broken bones or permanent injuries. I suspect because curiosity, excitement, creativity, and imagination at that point were stronger forces in my life than fear, tension, or stress, I landed on the concrete as relaxed as I had been on the roof above. At this point I was still ignorant of fear of physical injury. The lectures I would receive for that episode would instill that fear into my being, and that fear was most prominently pronounced in the weeks following as I struggled to learn to ride a bicycle without the training wheels.

I remember very little fear from the early years in doing. All fear was in thinking. I started kindergarten at the age of four. I remember waiting for the adults in my life to come and get me, and for whatever reason that I cannot remember they were late. I started home on my own. I felt no fear until half-way home when I had to make decisions as to which route would be best. I stood on the street and tried to decide, and then the fear set in, but as long as I was actually walking I was O.K. exploring my new world as I would a few years later explore the lot next door to my grandmother's house.

As I sat there on the front porch of my grandma's house I would recall my journey as if it were a dream. The adults in my life would brag about that episode for years to come, but I could not understand the wonder. I was simply doing the obvious, and it would be the first of a long series of acts of a child surviving.

Hide and seek was always one of my favorite games. I think that I enjoyed the mystery and intrigue inherent in that game. Sometimes at night my mother would turn out all the lights throughout the house and we would play hide and seek in the house. My favorite place to hide was always underneath the bed. As I always hid in the same place each time, I wonder how it is that my mama always had so much difficulty finding me.

That bed that I hid under was special to me. It used to be my grandma's bed before she died.

My baby brother, who sleep-walked most of his childhood, would continue to get up in the middle of the night and get into that bed, long after grandma had died. I guess there was a part of him that did not realize grandma was dead. I remember many episodes of my daddy bringing my brother back to his own bed in the middle of the night.

I used to lie awake at night waiting for my grandma to appear in the doorway. A part of me wanted to run into her arms. Another part of me wanted her to sit down and tell me stories, and there was a part of me that was a little afraid. So grandma simply stood there staring at me, longing for me, and missing me.

For whatever reason one night my baby brother was afraid of grandma. He saw her standing there in the doorway also and he was afraid. I don't really know why, other than I think I was closer to grandma than he was. I knew she would never hurt me, or so I thought, but I was less afraid than he. So I climbed from my top bunk bed into the bed below with my baby brother. I did that on several nights, but apparently I was not very good at making him feel better, so one night he yelled and screamed until my daddy came and made me get into my own bed. He got in bed with my brother. I can still hear my daddy's voice saying, "I don't think anything is going to get you while I'm here, you know I'm a pretty big fella." I felt a lot better because my daddy was a "pretty big fella".

After that night my grandmother stopped coming by to see us as often, and eventually I never saw her again. Although in my mind, I can still see her in that doorway in that same blue uniform that she used to wear to work every night to clean the post office. I guess after her death she was still used to staying up late at night since she worked from ten at night till six in the morning as I remember. Still, sometimes, every now and then although I can no longer see my grandmother I can still feel her staring at me from the doorway as I go to sleep.

My world changed after my grandma died. I don't really know how, but I know it changed.

I remember once sitting at our little children's kitchen table - me, my sister, and my brother. It was a Friday night and we were waiting for my daddy to come home from work with his pay-check so we could eat. We waited and waited and got very hungry. I remember looking at my mama out the corner of my eyes and wondering what was she going to do. I remember my stomach hurting and wanting to say something, but not knowing what to say and somehow being afraid to talk. I remember my baby brother complaining that he was hungry and getting louder as time went on and finally getting angry. In the past when he got angry he would go downstairs and ask grandma for food. Somehow, we always knew that grandma was there and would help us, but after her death, I didn't know who was going to take care of us or feed us when my daddy did not come home with his pay-check.

Not too long after I had fallen through the garage roof, my sister sustained her first real injury. She, I, my brother, and several friends were playing. We were jumping across sunken concrete stairs which led into the basement. It was wonderful fun, pushing, exploring, lunging, and leaping forward, testing the limits and strength of our young bodies. Several of us had made it across when my sister missed and fell onto the concrete below her teeth piercing through her bottom lip. She would be the first of the three of us to get stitches and would receive more stitches than any of us throughout childhood. I remember feeling rather guilty for some time to come every time I saw the stitch marks beneath my sister's lips.

I think from that day forward I realized that she was not as big as I, as strong as or as physically daring and confident as I. For the rest of childhood and the remainder of life, no matter where we were or what we were doing, I would always have this inner sense that a part of me needed to be looking out for my sister. We are both grown now and have been for some time, but every now and then I call her. Deep down, I know it is that little boy I once was who wants to ensure she never gets stitches again.

It seems that from my earliest memories of my father they have always been involved with the feelings of longing, wanting, and desiring. My daddy's favorite place when I was a child was a place named the Five "0" Lounge, or as he affectionately referred to it, the "Fifty Bar." I can remember many courageous trips I took in search of my daddy throughout the Five "0" Lounge. Each time I would seem to be filled with this fear that overwhelmed me and sought to destroy my mission. In retrospect, I think that my expeditions would have been easier if I had been old enough or tall enough to see over the bar. I can remember many days opening that huge door that seemed to weigh as much as I did and walking inside the smoke-filled room scared to death. I'm not sure what I was afraid of; all I know is I was scared. I remember walking from chair to chair asking, "You seen Pete Williams? Have you seen Pete Williams?"

The adults were big and tall and they sat on these tall stools that I had difficulty climbing up onto. I guess, in retrospect, I should be grateful. As I got older I grew to look more like my daddy. People would look at me and automatically say, "You're Pete's boy, aren't you?" This made my searching easier.

It was in front of the Fifty Bar that I learned an important lesson in life. I learned that I had the ability to do wrong. Before this incident I don't believe that it ever had occurred to me that I could do something wrong.

Being held in my daddy's arms had always been a respite for me. It was a place of sheer joy at just being me. It was in front of the Fifty Bar that I realized I had committed my first sin - although inadvert it may have been it was a sin none the less.

I stared up into my daddy's big brown eyes admiring his huge shoulders and arms and I said, "Daddy, pick me up." A bit louder the second time: "Daddy, pick me up." Finally, while tugging on his fingers: "Daddy, pick me up." He looked into my eyes and said, "Michael, no, you're getting too big to pick up," and I realized I had committed my first sin - I had grown. Until this day, I still remember the feeling that of a knife twisting and stabbing at my heart. I was utterly defenseless to protect myself from its sheer stabbing and jabbing as it laid me open to the cruel New Jersey wind on that gusty autumn day. Although I did not know it at the time, I think I felt my first feelings of jealousy that day. I was jealous of whatever he did at the Fifty Bar that put that glazed look in his eyes which he loved more than he loved me.

I don't remember ever asking my daddy to pick me up again. I would hold onto his fingers sometimes, or play in his hair, or gaze at him longingly, or when I became older rub my shoulder next to his, but I never again asked him to pick me up.

There is something I lost that day in front of the Five "0" Lounge that I have struggled to regain my entire life. That something was not small, just like I was no longer small. I lost my sense of innocence. That sense of lost innocence would accompany me throughout the next few years as my search for my daddy would take me through floating crap games, poker games, and more bars as the years progressed. In each place, I would always be greeted with the same salutation: "Hey, you're Pete's boy, aren't you?"

Searching for my daddy became a skill which the family would depend upon more as the years went by. I learned many things while searching for my daddy. I learned how to ride the bus system in New Jersey. I learned how to navigate the New York City subway system. I learned how to locate and enter a floating crap game without getting cut by the lookout. I learned how to get information from the drunks without their robbing me, and I learned how to develop a way out of every situation at the same time I was also developing a way in.

Exploring the lot next door to my grandma's house with its feelings of anticipation, excitement, magic, and enchantment gave way to exploring bars, gambling houses, and after-hours joints. The magic and enchantment gave way to stress, anxiety, and fear.

I would continue to search for my daddy in one way or another for the next three decades, finally losing him somewhere between Georgia and Tennessee, not knowing whether he was dead or alive. My skills were still as sharp as ever, however I had been beaten into surrender. I thereby accepted the sadness, pain, and desperation that are a part of never really having known ones' daddy.

The best Christmas I ever had I had at my grandma's house. The tree was magnificent. I was overwhelmed with its beauty. It reached to the ceiling four or five times my height. After my grandma's death we continued to place her favorite ornament at the top of the tree. This act on grandma's behalf made me feel better. In a strange way, it made me feel as if grandma was still there. During that time of the year my daddy's brothers would come over at one time or another. Although I was too young to realize it at the time, these men would later set the mark for that which I would long to become.

I remember well not being able to sleep at night and waking up several times wondering, "Had Santa been here yet?" I remember wondering how Santa got into our house since our chimney had concrete in it. My daddy did explain it to me but it was too complicated and I forgot.

Then during the night it happened. I heard Santa sneaking around and the noise of Santa leaving my presents woke me up. I was filled with joy and excitement and wanted to leap out of bed and fly down the steps to catch Santa in the act, and we would play and play and play and play. I was so happy and excited I felt that moment of anticipation was going to kill me. Then I heard hollering and screaming that confused and scared me. It was like a great trembling and nervousness coming over my body and centering in my arms, shoulders, head, and stomach. I walked down the stairs slowly, becoming more and more fearful the closer I got to the hollering and screaming which I now determined to be my mother's voice with another undetermined voice in the background. As I entered the living room I don't remember a lot but I do remember the sight of our beautiful, magnificent, wonderful Christmas tree turned over on the floor.

I looked for my grandma's ornament at the top and it was nowhere to be found, and I felt a sinking feeling in the pit of my stomach. The other undetermined voice was my Uncle James, who had earlier gone out for a "taste" with my daddy, and apparently, when they got home Uncle James fell into the Christmas tree and knocked it over.

I don't really know if Santa had come yet; I don't remember. I was so scared and upset by the whole ordeal, waking up, seeing the tree knocked over, losing my grandma's favorite ornament, and hearing my mama hollering and screaming and my daddy and uncle hollering back that I simply forgot to look for my presents.

They sent us back to bed and it was hard to go back to sleep. I think that I was nervous and confused. I'm not sure. The only thing that I was sure of is that I was scared. I was scared a lot.

The next morning, much to my surprise, Santa had come and he brought me a new bicycle too. I didn't even know that I wanted a bicycle until I saw it. It was beautiful and out of all the gifts I had ever gotten it was the best one ever.

This was the best Christmas I had throughout childhood. It was the one that I would remember the most. There was more magic and enchantment in that Christmas than in any other and the tree was prettier than any other. I think that it was the first Christmas since my grandma died.

That Christmas evening after dinner my daddy, mama, and the other adults in the house told stories and laughed at Uncle James and daddy getting drunk and knocking over the Christmas tree, but each time they would tell the story and laugh I would get nervous and get that sinking feeling in the pit of my stomach. I would re-hear the yelling and screaming from the night before. I would continue to get that sinking feeling in the pit of my stomach throughout the rest of childhood.

My daddy and uncles enjoyed Christmas about as much as I did, and I often had to beg for my toys. Sometimes I would sit in the corner and watch them play and I enjoyed that a lot. I loved watching my daddy and uncles.

CHAPTER 3

VIOLENCE IN CHILDHOOD

I admired that part of my siblings that allowed them to fight. As I remember I have never been a fighter. I think watching the fights between my mama and daddy repulsed me against fighting.

The first fight I remember between my baby brother and sister happened in the kitchen at my grandma's house. My brother got a handful of his older sister's hair and pulled it out. My sister had long reddish-brown hair flowing over head and shoulders; it was beautiful. The fight happened next to the washing machine with the hand wringer on it. I don't remember what the fight was about, but I do remember an immense sadness over it. Maybe I was sad because my brother and sister had joined the ranks of my mama and daddy. I felt alone in my fear, in my unwillingness to fight, and my confusion.

Later that unwillingness caused me pain. We were down the street in front of Mrs. Philpot's house when my siblings got in a fight with some kids. I watched my sister and brother kick ass and go from one kid to another without much resistance at all, each of them being voracious fighters. Later that evening when we returned home they reported to our parents their exploits. I who did not participate was left standing there in front of my parents. I had failed to prove myself in battle. Once again my Uncle James proved to be a pivotal part of my life as he laughed and taunted my parents that I must have been busy taking care of the biggest one the real bully in the group, which sounded like a reasonable explanation to me. I remember standing in front of my parents, my uncles, and siblings. I now realize I felt judged inadequate. As I look back on that day I believe I was paralyzed with fear at imposing injuries on other humans as I had seen my parents impose them on each other. I was afraid of the bloodshed I had seen, the screams I had heard, and the bruises I had witnessed. I felt useless.

After the whipping, my daddy gave me, my paralysis moved into a new arena. I would be afraid to commit violence against another human being and I would be afraid not to because of the violence that would be perpetrated upon me if I did not. I now had a new anxiety, knowing that I would be handed over to my daddy. That level of intense anxiety would revisit me each time I suspected my parents were about to fight. Would I have to choose sides? Which side was the right side? If I did not participate would I once again be considered not having proved my faithfulness to both?

As the years went on I would become a better and better fighter. I would have the experience of being knocked out by my mama, cut on the hand with a butcher knife by her, and knocking down my daddy. During other times, I would revert back, to my original position as peacemaker as I and my sister would struggle, pull, yell, scream, cry, catch their arms, or jump on their backs to separate the warring factions. I would handle one parent and my sister would handle the other. We would witness and be part of terrible acts of violence by the people we loved the most. Each blow delivered to the head, the arms, the shoulders, the back of a parent by a parent would eat at my heart and my soul, and that feeling of nervousness and overwhelming anxiety would become more profound.

I developed a sixth sense of my parents' ability to commit violence against me, my sister, my brother, or each other. I would lie awake at night afraid to go to sleep wondering what yell, what sound of flesh pounding against flesh would awaken me. I developed the ability to sense the minute emotional tremors that could erupt into a full-blown violent quake, and as these tremors increased in intensity so would my anxiety and my efforts to preempt the inevitable. I would lie in bed afraid that my daddy would not come home and afraid that my daddy would come home. The longing of my heart for his presence was in constant battle with the fear of the two of them to be together.

A quarter century later I would come to realize the full horror of growing up in that situation - waking up in the middle of the night yelling, screaming, and crying; as I had so often done in childhood. I was reliving one of my parents' many fights in yet another dream that I had lived in all too long. As if it were yesterday I can still see my daddy's fist coming down onto my mama's back. I can still hear the hollow sound the back makes when one is struck directly over the lungs. I can still see the terror in my sister's eyes as she struggled to get out of the way of the blow. I can still see my mama sink a little bit closer to the floor. I can still feel that sinking feeling in my stomach. I can still feel the powerlessness. I can feel the helplessness.

As my mother grabbed the butcher knife and attempted to drive it into my daddy's chest I can remember seeing the fear in my daddy's eyes as I stepped between the two of them and grabbed my mama's hand, allowing my own hand to be cut in the process. I can remember my sister and me wrestling with my mama's hand, struggling to remove the knife. I will never be able to adequately describe that one moment of fear.

As my daddy left the house that night I remember realizing he had been cut. Wiping up my daddy's blood from the floor is something I would do more than once during childhood but it is something that I would despise being forced to do for the remainder of my life. I hated not so much the chore itself; I think that I hated the feeling of having failed. I had failed to prevent the two people I loved the most from having hurt each other once again.

Somewhere deep within my heart there is a little boy still on his knees with a bucket of soapy, bloody water cleaning the floor of his daddy's blood while crying uncontrollably. I have failed in my efforts to console that child's tears as much as I have failed in my efforts to prevent those I loved the most from attempting to kill each other.

I don't often think back to those days. I spent most of my life making a conscious effort to forget but every now and then, if only for a fleeting moment, I remember. I remember being a crying little boy on his knees, in the middle of the floor, in the middle of the night, with that warm feeling of blood oozing down my arm as I sat there and just cried "God, please help me, God, please help me, God, please help me, God, please help me, please?"

Then twenty-five years later I wake up from this nightmare, yelling, screaming, crying, with the nurses and orderlies all flying into my room, I suddenly realized why they put safety bars on hospital beds and once again I am reliving the past in my dreams. Although one would not believe so if the sweat with which I was drenched was any indication. I would spend the next forty-eight hours crying uncontrollably and walking up and down the hospital floor, back and forth, and back and forth, attempting to walk away from this pain that had followed me for over twenty-five years and over a thousand miles from its origin. A nurse would inquire as to my pain and I would simply repeat again and again, "I should have killed him when I had the chance, I should have killed him when I had the chance."

CHAPTER 4

CHILDHOOD SPIRITUALITY

My grandmother died on April 7th and I made my first communion on May 13th.

I was dressed up in my white suit and shoes and felt rather special. I remember thinking that I was going to feel something special. As I knelt at the altar and partook of my first communion, I was genuinely interested in being whatever God wanted. I guess God wanted me to be sad, because my strongest feeling of first communion was coming outside St. Mary's Church and being overwhelmed by a sense of loss. My grandmother was not there to share that moment. What I remember most was missing and longing for my grandmother.

My life took on a form of emptiness after my grandmother's death, like a hole in the pit of my stomach. Life had lost its enchantment. Things that I used to do that had genuinely brought joy to my heart now brought partial smiles. There was a delight I had taken in myself while grandma was alive that I could not regain.

Sometimes I used to do things purely to shock or amaze grandma. The first childhood rhyme I ever learned I think served just that purpose. "Beans, beans, good for your heart. The more you eat the more you fart. Jack didn't know the beans were loaded; threw off the covers, threw off the sheets; made a fifty-yard dash for the toilet seat." Grandma hated that but she also smiled.

I learned to worry after grandma died. I remember listening to the women, my mama talked to as she was trying to decide whether to take my daddy back, and that worried me a lot. She accused him of killing grandma and that confused me.

Then there was Mr. Seymour. He lived downstairs in the basement of my grandmother's house. Sometimes I heard my mama say that had Mr. Seymour called an ambulance, grandma would still be alive, and I vaguely remember something about coal gas. All I know is that I was confused. Mr. Seymour died soon thereafter. I didn't know Mr. Seymour well. He was a small, light-skinned man who I remember sometimes walked with a cane. What I remember most about Mr. Seymour was that when he died and my mother finally located his family she called one of his sons and that son had said, "Why are you calling me?" I remember that because my mama talked about it a lot and about what a terrible man he must have been and a horrible father. I remember feeling sorry for Mr. Seymour.

I think the first angry feelings I ever felt toward my mama was during this time when she compared my father to Mr. Seymour. Somehow, I intuitively knew that she blamed my father for her mother's death, that she was angry that he stole the five hundred dollars and that he had disappeared for so long, and that he was never there for her. Maybe I did not realize all these things on a conscious level but I believe they reflected themselves in my psyche, because somehow her anger at him felt O. K. in a strange sort of way, although scary as it may have been. When she talked about how her mother would still be alive today had my father not stolen the five hundred dollars, there was a strange sort of softness, honesty, or vulnerability about her ravings, but when she predicted how I and my siblings would feel about my daddy if he did not change his ways I felt different. Ignorant of my own feelings at the time, I realized later that I felt manipulated and controlled. Somehow, as she ranted and raved about how we the children would one day feel about my daddy, I became reduced, no longer a little boy with my own feelings, ranting, and ravings, which I did have, but somehow I became an object to be used against my daddy.

I think that my anger or uncomfortable feelings stemmed from the fact that I felt completely different about my daddy than she represented. I loved him, I admired him, I adored him, I longed to be with him, and I worshipped him. I had this attachment towards him that I had toward no other since my grandmother's death. Strange as it may seem, I think this attachment grew out of one act. Occasionally, my daddy would lay his hand on the top of my head and say, "How you doing, Slim?" I longed for this act of kindness, of love, and of affection. I would maneuver my way through situations, people, and places for the opportunity to stand within reach of my daddy's large, strong, muscular hand; waiting, hoping, and praying for the fatherly touch, the firm grip and the obligatory, "How you doing, Slim?" Most of the time I felt completely invisible to not only my daddy but to both of my parents and most of the adults in my life, but when my father grabbed me by the top of my head and said, "How you doing, Slim?" I felt like someone knew that I was there. I was alive. I was a human being and it felt good.

I gravitated toward my daddy because of this act. It was the closest thing that I received resembling the attention that my grandmother used to give me, and I longed for that sort of attention again from anybody. When my daddy grabbed me by the top of my head, that act sparked the part of me that wanted to climb up in someone's lap and simply cry, cry, cry, "My grandma's dead, my grandma's dead, my grandma is gone."

There is no place I loved in the house more than the staircase leading to the second floor. Sometimes I would sit on those stairs for hours just thinking. Later on as I learned about books, the staircase was my favorite place to enjoy them. Sometimes my curiosity led me to things that I will always remember. I had been wondering how light-bulbs worked and why. I think I asked my daddy a little bit about it, but it was too complicated, so I set out to explore. I took the bulb out of the socket over the staircase and explored. Then, deciding that I needed to know what electricity felt like, I stuck my finger into the socket, which was O. K. until I pulled the switch. Wow, what a shock, and until this day, I can still remember the very unique sensation of electricity coursing through my body. Luckily, I instinctively pulled away, but the sensations continued and I believe I was a little bit dazed. I was lectured by my parents for this but I believe they thought it was funny. I never stuck my finger in that light socket again, but I would continue to sit on that staircase.

As I remember it, my grandmother spent a lot of time on the first floor and my parents spent most of their time on the second floor.

As I look back on that part of my life, I believe that my sitting on that staircase was a metaphor for where I was in my heart. I was midway between being my grandma's baby and my parents' child. I was unable to let go of my grandmother and unable to hold onto my parents. I would sit on that staircase and I would miss my grandma, and as time went by, I would contemplate how to get my parents' attention. In retrospect, I suspect sticking my finger in that socket was a way to get their attention because I was angry.

I was angry my grandmother had died and I was no longer anyone's baby. I was angry that no one gazed into my eyes anymore and reflected wonder, enchantment, and amazement. I was angry that no one whispered in my ear anymore, but most of all, more than anything, I was angry that no one held me to their breast anymore, no one caressed me anymore, and no one protected me anymore. For the first time in my life, I was discovering what it felt like to be alone, alone in my sadness, alone in my desperation, and alone in my guilt.

A few weeks before my grandmother's death she had given me the only spanking I would ever receive from her. I was shocked and angry, and, unlike many people I have known over the course of my life, I have never learned to appreciate anyone laying their hands on me. After my grandmother spanked me, I had wished that she was dead and soon thereafter, she was. In addition to all the other things, I was confused about at the time I was overwhelmed by this sense of guilt which I had to learn to live with. This may not have been the first time I felt guilt in my life but it was definitely the most profound and intense for years to come.

The staircase leading to the basement had many opposite feelings for me. Mr. Seymour had lived in the basement. Also, the furnace was located there. It was my responsibility for some time to come to start the furnace in the afternoon, when we got home from school. It was not much of a responsibility once one got the hang of it, but there is a definite art to stoking a coal furnace. I always hated the job. When I look back on those days, though, I realize that I got a lot of praise from my parents for the good job that I did, but I did not do it for their praise, I did it more than anything because I hated seeing my sister and brother cold more than I hated stoking the furnace. For a long time I resented having to do that.

I believe I hated it because it made me confront my fears. I had to pass Mr. Seymour's old room in order to get to the furnace. I also had to go into the basement first before I could turn on the light, which meant I had to enter into the dark. It was a responsibility that had to be met adequately, unlike my mediocre dish-drying with my grandma; this had to be done right. I was constantly afraid I would screw it up, which I did on several occasions when the furnace would go out and we had no heat. The basement represented my fear of inadequacy and my fear of death compounded with darkness. If my sitting on the upstairs staircase was a metaphor for where I was in my heart, midway between being my grandmother's baby and my parents' child, then the downstairs staircase was a metaphor for where I had been and what I was becoming. I had been an enchanted child who once believed in magic and I was becoming afraid. I was afraid of death, darkness, responsibility, and inadequacy.

Unlike the upstairs staircase where I would sit and think, I only stood at the top of the downstairs staircase attempting to muster the courage to do what had to be done. I would pray to my grandma to protect me while I did what had to be done. I would enter the basement slowly one step at a time, and once the furnace work was completed, I would slam the furnace door and fly down the hallway and up the stairs as fast as I could before anything or anyone got me.

I wish that I could run into my parents' arms as fast as I can but they have their own problems. Daddy's drinking and he stole the five hundred dollars from grandma. Mama and daddy might break up, Mama still thinks that daddy is responsible for grandma's death. She talks about him bad when he is not around. I really wish that my grandma was still alive so that I would have someone to take care of me, hold me, and protect me.

CHAPTER 5

DIFFERENT WORLDS IN CHILDHOOD

If there was one source of wonder, enchantment, and amazement that has never eluded me, it was within the world of books. I learned to mesmerize myself within the world of books, to go where the characters went; to live their lives, and to realize their exploits.

Still till this day, I can marvel at the wonderful exploits that I immersed myself in at the time of Pecos Bill, John Henry, Paul Bunyan, and Gulliver's Travels and Peter Pan my favorites. When I was younger I would ask my mother to read these stories to me. As I got better at reading I would read these stories to myself, over and over again. I especially liked Peter Pan because I identified with Tinker Bell. I wanted to be Tinker Bell and fly, fly away, with no worries, no ills and live in a land where little boys never grew up and eventually all would be well.

I felt like Gulliver in Gulliver's Travels. I identified with that part of Gulliver that had to be tied down and restrained by the little people. I had this great empathy for Gulliver because he had been restrained and tied down, and I felt I knew what that felt like, so I would read that part of the story again and again. I would sit on the staircase midway between being my grandma's baby and my parents' child and I would read and retreat into my own world where I was neither, where what I could be was limited only by what I could read, and I could read a lot. In my world of books there were no adults whom I had to depend upon or who would hurt me, and if I did not like a world I could simply grab another book. In this world of books I had the freedom to be who I wanted to be, as opposed to who I needed to be to satisfy the adults around me. In this world I was little boy king.

As the years progressed I retreated into that world deeper and deeper, and in a sense I have never left. Strange as it may seem, this is a world that my mother not only exposed me to, but quite literally forced me into. She gave a precious gift. I had difficulty learning to read and to correctly pronounce certain words. For a while, I think they suspected I might be retarded. The first school I ever was affiliated with was Seton Hall University where they tried to teach me to speak correctly. As I look back on those days I often suspect that I was smarter than I let on and smarter than all the adults around me suspected. My difficulty in learning how to read and lack of understandable speech was simply my way not to participate in the world around me. The adult world was scary and violent and full of all kinds of things that I was unsure of, so I simply refused to enter this world. I refused to fully admit its existence. I was much safer in my own world where, lonely as it may be, at least it was quiet, peaceful, and serene. I would sit in corners for hours at a time and stare at the walls or play with my marbles. Over time my mother actually grew to accept and admire this part of my personality and would brag to her friends about what a good and quiet child I was. In my world I could sit and dream about the days when my grandma was alive, the days when I used to be little boy king. In my world there was no stealing, no anger, no death, no violence, and, most of all, no uncertainty. In my world, I was safe, completely safe from the adults around me. In my world I was king.

One day when my mother was attempting to teach me and my siblings to read, she became very frustrated. Each time I stumbled on a word she would hit me upside the head, which really hurt. I can feel the sting of her wedding ring smashing into my skull. Maybe deep down inside she knew that I was smarter than I let on, maybe not. The point is I started to read better and better because I was afraid of being hit. I was more afraid of being hit again and again than I was afraid of entering into this adult world of speech, language, and stories, and so I started to read. It was and is probably one of the most miraculous confrontations of fear I have ever had. I say that only because of the wonderful world it exposed me to -the world of books, stories, and imagination. In one respect my mother forced me out of one fantasy world and into another and both I would learn to retreat into as time progressed.

The struggle of my childhood was not only a struggle of reality, but it was a struggle to seek some form of relief from reality. It was a struggle for emotional rest.

My world of books and my world of quiet solitude without speech or human contact became my best friends. I became my own best friend, the only one I could trust and the only one who would get me out of many situations that would continually worsen as the years went on. I would learn how to sit in a corner and disappear for hours on end, never being noticed by anyone. My parents would applaud my quiet, my solitude, and my ability never to get on their nerves.

At this point in my childhood I received few spankings. I realized very early one could not be spanked if one could not be seen. I don't really know when the verbal attacks began. I do know that I had internalized my parents' negative feelings about me by the fourth grade. I sat on the right side of the classroom at the very front. One of my best friends at the time was Gregory, a light-skinned, dark curly haired, heavy set little boy who for whatever reason I do believe loved me. The teacher had left the room, and the longer she was gone the more kids in the room started to talk, play, and have fun until practically most of the room was involved.

When the nun in her black habit and white bib returned she went to her desk and grabbed her ruler and advised the class that everyone who had been talking would be swatted on the hand. She requested all the children who had talked while she was gone to hold out their hands. She went through the room swatting children's hands with that wooden ruler as hard as she could. The sound of the ruler swatting their flesh rang in my ears over and over until I could hardly stand it. The sound reminded me of that sound of flesh pounding against flesh that I had so often heard at home. Once again my stomach got that sinking feeling again and I became overwhelmed with nervousness and anxiety. I wanted to bust out of my seat and run out of that room as fast as I could and never stop running.

As she proceeded up and down the rows, she finally got to me and I held out my hand and she swatted me: "swat" and again "swat." Gregory, who sat next to me in the next row, jumped out of his seat and hollered. "Sister, sister, no, he didn't talk, he didn't talk." She looked at me and stared into my eyes and said, "Were you talking?" I looked at her and said "yes" and she proceeded to swat me.

I never uttered a word, that day, but I felt there was something about me that needed to be beaten, punished, and destroyed. When she asked me if I talked that day, in my mind I knew that I had not, but when she asked, it was like she was asking me was I good or bad and I believed myself to be bad. Therefore I deserved to be beaten. In my mind, I could not conceive of a situation where people were being beaten when I would not deserve to be beaten also. I think that this was the birth of my self-destructive tendencies.

As Gregory jumped from his seat to declare my innocence, I remember feeling very awkward and confused. I think I felt that deep down inside he did not know how bad I really was. Although every teacher I ever had throughout grammar school would say the same thing, "Michael daydreams a lot," fourth grade is really the first time I actually remember daydreaming in school. I would look out the window and simply dream. I loved to dream. In my dream world there was peace, there was certainty, and there was quiet. In my dream world there was grandma or at least some resemblance of the way it was before grandma died.

It's peculiar the way childhood works. I was told certain things over and over and some of it I never believed. Then one day it happens and it sinks in and it becomes truth. My parents had called me stupid hundred of times, in the early years. But I never believed them until the fifth grade. I was sitting there trying to follow this math problem that the teacher was explaining on the board, and for whatever reason I just couldn't get it. She explained it again and again, but I couldn't get it.

Then it occurred to me. "Oh my God, my parents are right, I am stupid!" Suddenly that sinking feeling in the pit of my stomach was lower than it had ever been before. There was this sudden realization that I may as well not try. That I was never going to be successful. Through no fault of my own I was just stupid. I never again would regain that sense of confidence that I had about myself before that moment of stark realization. I think that it was important to accept my parents' perception of me. I needed and wanted for my parents to be right not only about their perceptions of me but about all things.

My parents' were Gods, all-knowing and wise about all things. I think that I needed for them to be that because that would bring some measure of certainty and safety in my world, even if the things they were right about were things that I would have preferred to be otherwise.

What I wanted and what I needed were always at war with what I wanted and what I needed. I wanted and needed to be smart bright and the apple of my parents' eye, but I also wanted and needed my parents to be right. So I settled for them to be right about all things and at whatever cost, even if that cost be me. I learned to sacrifice myself for what was wanted and needed by the adults around me. I learned to hurt, to despair, and to seek my own destruction in a myriad of ways.

CHAPTER 6

ORCHARD BEACH, FUN, AND PAIN

Some of the most delightful times of my childhood were spent together as a family at Orchard Beach in New York. My mama would make potato salad with plenty of eggs in it. There would be all kinds of thermos bottles of Kool-Aid, potato chips, and other stuff, but I could live off of my mama's potato salad and Kool-Aid.

I would get really excited the night before, and sometimes mama would let me sleep in my swimming trunks so I would be ready to go as soon as I got up. We would wake up early. First, we would go to New York to pick up my uncle, aunt, and cousins who were already in New York near Amsterdam Ave. and 125th Street. From there, off to the beach we would go. Sometimes I would fall asleep before we got there, but I would always wake up when we got near the water. There was something about the smell of saltwater that would always wake me up. I loved how the scenery would change the closer we got, with trees and all sorts of things that we never saw in Newark.

The smell of the saltwater awoke many senses in me which were rarely touched - adrenalin seemed to surge against my veins much like the ocean tide surges against the shore, which by now I would be dying to see. The closer we got to the water the more excited I became until I was overwhelmed with excitement. By the time my daddy parked the car I would want to run as fast as I could through the parking lot, onto the beach, over the sand and into the water.

Unfortunately, we always had to unload the car first. Food, coolers, beach chairs, blankets, they all had to be carried onto the beach, and most importantly my and my siblings, plastic pails, and shovels whereby we would move, shape, and again move and reshape huge amounts of sand over the course of the day.

I loved being in the water more than anything, especially when the tide was coming in and the huge waves with their white gushing water would sometimes be so strong that I could actually ride them. I remember my first experience of eating sand and sea weed and pondering such questions as, "What makes the little bubbles in the seaweed" or "why is the water inside sea weed always saltier than regular sea water." I think that I may have first bonded with my baby brother at the beach. We would wrestle in the water for hours on end, seeing who could throw the other on his backside. This experience was more fun because of the waves that would submerge us both from time to time. I would pick my brother up and throw him into the water and every now and then, I would also allow him to throw me into the water, never revealing that I was stronger than he was. Being a big brother is a responsibility. I learned early that strength is something that sometimes should be relinquished and always used expeditiously. I intuitively knew he loved the feeling and the exhilaration of being able to throw his big brother on his backside. I think this relinquishment of strength was one of the first times I realized that there could be joy in losing and watching another human being have the opportunity to win.

My sister, on the other hand, deserved a higher degree of care for she was never quite as comfortable in the water as we were. Although I can remember many occasions swimming submerged and attacking her legs from underneath as she would laugh and giggle while running back to shore screaming, "Mama make them leave me alone".

There is a magic about the ocean and when I am really quiet I can still hear my brother's and sister's laughter intermingled with my own and the rush of the waves crashing against the shore and my mama's voice in the background hollering from not to far off: "Aren't you kids tired yet?" as I, my sister, and brother all cried out in unison. "Just ten more minutes, just ten more minutes, please," as my mother conceded yet one more time.

We would have done anything to stay in the water, and it is probably the only thing from childhood that I am sure all of us adored. That sinking feeling in the pit of my stomach which was my constant companion throughout childhood would all but disappear during the time that I was in the water. I hated that sinking feeling. I would have done anything to get rid of it. As I became older and studied geography, I would eventually realize that on the other side of the Atlantic Ocean there were actually countries. I would sit on the beach with the sun on my back and I would daydream about this England on the other side of the Atlantic that I had read about in school.

That daydream became one of my favorites, although in reality, I would have preferred to have been any place other than where I was when my parents were arguing and fighting with each other, so I would dream. Little did I realize at the time that about a quarter of a century later I would one day actually get on a plane and travel to England! The land I had dreamed about as a child that was across the ocean, that I would one day run away to, to get rid of the pain that I carried inside in growing up in a home riddled with violence. I would have gone anywhere, done anything to leave that pain behind.

There was this small island which sat just off Orchard Beach maybe about a quarter mile or so off shore. I would watch my daddy and uncle swimming toward that island and I would envy their strength and stamina to swim that far. I would dream of the day when I would be a man and do such as they did, with their large manly shoulders rising just above the water. Watching them was good for me I do believe. My thoughts of that island with its grass just past the shoreline are with me till this day, although I never sat foot on it. I dreamed of one day swimming to it and being with my daddy and uncle. Men, doing manly stuff, and therefore claiming my independence, my strength, and my resilience. At a very young age I believed that manhood was not something to grow into but something that is earned.

Twenty-five years later as I flew over the island on my way to England I would remember that island and I would remember my childhood dreams. I would re-hear my siblings' laughter. I would feel the gush of the waves splashing against my young body once again. I would remember the taste of seaweed. I would long for my family whom I yearned to be with and so desperately wanted to escape from.

I would re-live that sinking feeling in the pit of my stomach and I would cry. I would cry the same tears that I cried as a child and for the exact same reasons. Sometimes life has no point, it just is.

CHAPTER 7

STARING INTO MY FAMILIES EYES

My first trip to Georgia was a truly wondrous event. I can remember my parents planning days ahead. This would be my first time meeting my daddy's father and mother. I was quite excited about the opportunity. It may have also been my mother's first opportunity to meet my daddy's parents, I don't really know.

My siblings, my parents, some of my uncles, and I were all in two cars: my grandma's 1957 Chevrolet and my uncle Bob's Cadillac. We headed straight down I-95, otherwise known as the New Jersey Turnpike, down the entire east coast of the country straight into Georgia. Until this trip I never knew there were two parts of the country. One part was North and the other part South. Apparently we lived in the North and the South part had something to do about the Mason-Dixon Line, which apparently was somewhere between Baltimore and Washington, D.C. Once you went past it you were in the South.

This trip was my first real lesson in geography, but also my first real lesson in humanity or the lack thereof. Until this trip, I may not have realized I was black. I guess it just had never yet been that important. I remember my parents and my uncles prior to the trip discussing whether we would be able to get a room in a hotel or motel. Apparently, they thought it might be difficult for my siblings and me to ride the entire trip with no break. From what I could tell, there were these hotel or motel things, but they were not something that were readily available to black folks. I remember one of my uncles saying that he thought Howard Johnson's would take black folks and then another saying that even Howard Johnson's would not take black folks below Baltimore. I remember thinking to myself that this Mr. Johnson sure was a peculiar guy to do one thing in one place and something different in another place.

My uncle Bob finally said we would drive straight through without stopping, that it didn't make sense taking any chances and we would save time.

Although she never said anything, I remember sensing my mother's fear during this time. I was not real sure what she was afraid of, but I remember being afraid because she was afraid. It would be years before I would be able to conclude that because my mother was born and raised in New Jersey, for her going to this land of segregation for the first time would be scary. She made a whole lot of sandwiches and fried chicken so we would have plenty to eat, since no one was sure if they would serve food to black folks at Mr. Johnson's. I remember having a lot of fun during this trip. I liked watching my uncles. I also remember not being able to stay awake long. It seemed like every time we got in the car I would fall asleep. I do remember seeing my first Howard Johnson's as we drove by it on the highway, because I asked my daddy to show me one. Wow, was it big. I figured this Mr. Johnson was probably some kind of guy.

I remember the first sign I ever saw that said "coloreds." We had stopped for gas and in this gas station there was the white folks' bathroom and the coloreds' folks bathroom. Also there was the white folks' water fountain and the coloreds' folks water fountain. I remember my parents being real concerned because my sister drank the white folks' water. I just thought she was thirsty. She always did like water. I like Kool-Aid myself. One of the white men at the gas station was really upset with my daddy because my sister drank their water. He started saying some things that did not sound very friendly to me. Then I realized my daddy got scared so I got scared also. My daddy rounded everyone up really quick and we left there in a hurry. As one of my uncles commented, "We better get the hell out of here now!"

My sister never did get any explanation as to why or how she had done anything wrong, but somehow afterward all of us kids knew that it better not happen again. My grandma had always taken water with her medicine, so I figured these white folks in the South somehow must be pretty poorly if they needed special water. I didn't want to be the cause of any white folks or any other kind of folks up and dying or getting sickly, so I made it a point not to drink any of their water, but I remember wondering how much fun this trip was going to be if all these folks in the South were poorly.

When we arrived at my grandparents' house it was dark. It was an old wooden house with a dirt yard off a dirt road and across the street from a cemetery. The first time I laid eyes on my daddy's mother was a magical moment. I stared into her eyes almost forever; I could not take my eyes away from hers. I was unable to move, to speak, or to act. It felt like I was staring into her eyes, my daddy's eyes, and my own all at the same time. I remember thinking to myself that she looked more like my daddy than anyone I had ever seen. At that moment I was reliving my family's history, becoming a part of that history and gaining a part of myself that I was unfamiliar with.

As I watched my grandmother peruse her sons, I was amazed. Uncle Bob she knew right away. She hugged him and she was happy. I remember being confused as I realized that she did not recognize all of her sons, but what I remember more than anything was when she looked at my daddy and asked, "Who's this big fella over here?" I think it was Uncle James or Uncle George who looked at her and said, "Muh dear, you don't know who that is? That's Peter," and my grandmother just grinned and grinned as she lunged at him.

It would not be until many years later that I would understand that it was years between family visits. I suspect that is why she was unable to recognize all of her sons. Having laid eyes on this set of grandchildren for the first time amazed her, but I could tell she was amazed at laying eyes on her own children more; and I as a young child was enthralled. I am not real sure what I saw that day, but what I think I saw was my grandmother expressing that same amazement toward her own children that my other grandmother used to express toward me.

The red clay of Georgia was certainly different from New Jersey, and I would have my first experience of being scared by a goat and running across the yard for safety. I would later learn that was a billy goat and they could be mean. I would see my first cows, my siblings and I referred to as monkeys, which seemed to delight the adults among us. I would meet my daddy's oldest sister, Eula-Dee, and my sister, Yvonne, would refer to one of our relative's home as a barn, causing all the adults to all tell her to shut up. I would see my first wood-burning stove and chew my first tobacco from my grandfather, which was not a pleasant experience. I don't remember as much about my grandfather as I do my grandmother. I would learn that my grandfather had the same name as my daddy and brother - they all were named Peter.

My grandmother was a very short brown-skinned woman with short hair who drank Black Label beer all day long and never wore shoes. On occasion, when I was playing in the front yard she would call me to the porch and ask, "Now who do you belong to?" I would reply, "My daddy's name is Peter," and she would say, "Oh yeah," as I grinned from ear to ear. For whatever reason I think she sometimes thought we belonged to Uncle George.

My grandfather would sit on the front porch and drink vodka from a water glass all day long, and once I mistakenly thought it was water and drank it, then I coughed real hard and choked.

It always felt good to me whenever my grandmother asked, "Now who do you belong to?" I think it felt good because somehow on some level I knew she was trying to figure out her connection to me, to hold onto that connection, to cherish it, and thus hold onto and cherish me. I think when she asked me that question several times a day, at that point she and I were very similar. I would look at her and my daddy together and try to figure out that connection. How was she related to me? Maybe that's why the first time I laid eyes on her I was unable to move, to speak, or to act. I simply stared in a trance. Maybe she and I both were desperately trying to bridge a gap of a thousand miles, quite a number of years, North and South, and filling it the best way we could. Maybe that's why I remember so vividly staring into her eyes, maybe I was trying to transcend time and space.

It was a wonderful experience seeing my daddy with his parents. There was this quality of innocence, vulnerability, and tentativeness about him that I had never seen before. I don't know why, but I do know seeing my father with his parents made me love him more.

He and I would walk to the store around the corner on the dirt path and dirt sidewalks to get my grandmother's beer several times a day, and I would wonder if he did this when he was a little boy. I think that for the first time in my young life during those walks to the store I thought of my father as a friend. He was going because his mama told him to, but I suspect he was also going because he wanted, to just as I was going just because I wanted to. We were little boys together.

It did not occur to me what the sign "whites only" or "no coloreds"' really meant until one day when we were riding down the street and passed a swimming pool. I saw all of the kids running, jumping, playing, and all of a sudden my heart skipped a beat. I wanted to run and jump into the water and play. Finally, I had found a part of Georgia just like New Jersey, and I couldn't wait to throw my siblings onto their backsides while in the water. My brother screamed as he saw the pool, "Mama, mama, I want to go swimming," as my sister and I joined in the pleading.

That's when it happened. My daddy said, "We can't go swimming." My brother continued to cry, "Why not, Please, daddy, can't we go swimming?" My daddy said, "No," once again. My brother continued to cry out "Daddy why not, daddy, why not?" My father then became angry and he said, "We can't go because were black." My daddy made a very curt attempt at explaining why we couldn't go swimming, and we just begged and pleaded all the more.

My father got angry that day. I believe my mother was frustrated and I was hurt. I didn't know what this being black meant. I was unable to connect our water fountain experience and Howard Johnson's to what was now going on. I do remember being in the car, riding past the pool, and seeing all the other kids playing, and being sad and hurt. I did know that if being black meant that I couldn't go swimming, then I really didn't want to be black. I wanted to be whatever I had to be in order to go swimming. I got angry with my parents that day. I couldn't understand why they would make me something which meant I couldn't go swimming.

CHAPTER 8

WHAT IS HOME TO A CHILD ?

My grandmother's neighborhood had held a lifetime of magic for me. Most of my best childhood memories occurred right there in that house at Seventy-Eight Wickliffe Street in Newark, New Jersey, and I would discover that to leave that house would be just one more scary event from childhood.

I had heard that when they tore it down, it took one hit with a wrecking ball and the entire house shattered. As the house fell in on itself and the dust flew upward, outward, and then settled to reveal the ruin, I wonder if the men doing the work knew that my grandma had lived there, that she died there, or that she whispered in my ear as I dried the dishes there. A concrete parking garage now occupies that city block. As I stood there leaning on the telephone pole that is the only remaining remnant of my first home, I remembered many other times shielding my eyes and leaning against that very same pole as my siblings the other neighborhood kids, Karen, Linda, Norman, and Gloria and I played hide and seek.

Although I was grown, I couldn't figure out how or why I was drawn to visit this concrete parking garage. I suspect because it was the first place I was loved and in many respects the best place I was loved. We would move to a different part of town. I think my parents thought it was a better neighborhood, but I didn't know what was wrong with the old neighborhood. The day we moved my daddy's brothers showed up to move us. Some of them were drunk, and my uncle George dropped the television and broke it, which made my mother very angry. I remember running back and forth from the truck to the house and from the house to the truck. I was very excited about this challenge to empty the house and fill up this huge truck.

I don't remember a lot about that day, but I do remember being in my grandmother's 1957 Chevrolet getting ready to go to our new home. I felt like I was leaving my grandmother all over again. I recalled her funeral, her burial, and blowing air into her face in my vain attempt to save her from death. That night as I was to sleep for the first time in our new house I would dream of grandma. It would not be until a couple of days later that the reality of the move would dawn on me: I was not going back to the old neighborhood and everyone and everything I had known my whole life was there.

I felt anxiety before the move and sadness after; I do not know which was worst. I did like our new house. The house was two stories with a wonderful balcony, which I would grow to love, and it had ivy growing all up some of the walls.

I didn't like this new neighborhood as well as I liked the old one. The old neighborhood was close to downtown, in fact just a couple of blocks away from city hall, and I could walk to almost anywhere I needed to go, including the Fifty Bar to get to see my daddy. In the new neighborhood I had to take the bus more and I did not like that. I didn't see my daddy as much after we moved to the new neighborhood. He spent a lot of time at the Fifty Bar down on Howard Street, but often I would go down and see him and spend time with him and that made me very happy. All of the people in the bar knew me, and if he wasn't there I could usually track him down, and I was always greeted with the same, "Hey, you're Pete's boy, aren't you?"

Sometimes I would sit on the stool next to my daddy while he had a taste, and he would always introduce me to his friends. I think he was very proud of me and the people used to always say that I looked just like him, that he must have "spit me out." I think I liked the fact that he must have "spit me out."

Some of my daddy's friends scare me, but I never say anything. These are the same people I will need when I can't find him. Although I am sometimes scared, it is worth it just to get a chance to be with my daddy, and I love it when he grabs me by the top of my head and tells me to do something. For whatever reason, after the move I think that I needed my daddy more.

It was about this time that I started looking for him in more varied places. Sometimes I would just walk through downtown or ride the bus to different places, hoping that I would catch a glimpse of him, especially during those times when he would disappear. Sometimes I would just hang out on the corner, the same corner where I discovered that I had grown too big to be picked up, and I would wait around for him to show up. Other times I would just walk the neighborhood to find out what was going on and how I might find him. I taught myself how to use the city bus system with no other hopes, thoughts, or aspirations than to be able to find my daddy. At times when I could not track him down, at least it would give me time to be alone and think. Sometimes I would miss him so much as I was riding the bus and looking out of the windows that I would stare at each man I saw on the streets to see if it might be my daddy.

My nightmares got worse after we moved to the new house. I used to have the same nightmare repeatedly. I was always being chased by this terrible monster who was right on my heels breathing fire that I could feel on the back of my neck, back, hands, and body. I would run as fast as I could, but no matter how fast I ran I could feel the heat getting hotter and painfully burning my flesh. I could feel the monster overtaking me, seeking to kill, to destroy, and to consume me whole, and I was afraid. I was completely consumed in this life and death struggle, which I knew I was losing. On some level I felt like I could handle this, which I guess was crazy. What threw me into terror was that as I ran I would scream as hard as my young lungs would allow. I would open my mouth as wide as humanly possible, and as I did I would immediately realize that nothing came out. My cries for help were muffled, smothered, and the harder I screamed the more nothing came out. I would scream these silent screams until the terror would consume me and I would wake up cold, trembling, and shaking. As the years progressed I learned to cope with my fears, but that same nightmare would haunt me throughout childhood and into my adult life for years to come.

I think that I grew closer to my mama after the move. We would sit up into the wee hours of the morning and watch movies. It seemed that she was always on one diet or another and would snack on things like cantaloupe, grapefruit, yogurt, or some form of canned fruit, and until this day, I still have a taste for all those things because of the many midnight snacks that I shared with my mother. My mother was always the epitome of responsibility and structure. I guess it was difficult for her during that time with my daddy's drinking and everything. We would sit up and talk for hours, and many of these conversations were about my daddy. I would listen intently to her tales and worries about my daddy, and sometimes we would have the same conversations repeatedly concerning my daddy's drinking. It was almost as if she was obsessed by him? The tone of her voice will forever ring in my ears: "Your father is a drunk, your father is no good, and when you grow up I want you to be anything but like your father."

I love my mother very much. I listen to her every night for what seems like all night. I wish that I could do more to help her. I do listen and I give advice when I can, but sometimes I get sleepy, but I am afraid to go to sleep. I cannot fall asleep. I need to be awake to separate them if my daddy comes home. Sometimes she goes to bed, but I stay awake looking at television. But sometimes I fall asleep sitting upright in the kitchen chair. I catch myself as my head starts to drop and the force of my head dropping wakes me up. Sometimes I can no longer hang on, and I fall asleep with my head in my arms at the kitchen table. Then I wake up in terror and jump, but it is O.K., it is just the television getting louder with a commercial.

Maybe they'll fight again tonight. I am afraid to even think the thought to let it enter my mind. With all the energy at my command I refuse to think the thought. I refuse to go to sleep. Good, another episode of Jackie Gleason. I like Jackie Gleason but it makes me nervous when he says that he's going to send Alice to the moon. Maybe because my mama's name is Alice.

I sit there watching television, refusing to think the thought, never letting the idea that the two people I love the most might attempt to kill each other again.

My efforts are pointless, meaningless, and without purpose. I sit up every night just to sit up. Soon it is a habit, a tradition, and an image as to the way I am, and I cannot break out. Its hold is too strong. So I sit there each night simply because it is what I do. I learn to love the night. It is quiet, no constant voices, demands, worries, and ills. I think that I like the peace, I like the quiet. Occasionally, I walk out to the balcony. I tell myself it is because I like the air, the wind in my face, and I do. Each time I see a man walking down the street from the direction my daddy usually comes from; I get excited, but also nervous, anxious, and scared all at the same time. It is not him, and I return to my kitchen chair. My sister's room is right off the kitchen, and I turn down the volume on the television. It is late. I start to nod again. I am somewhere between consciousness and sleep, stuck in the middle, unable to commit myself to either. It seems like a lot of my childhood is like that, stuck in the middle, but I survive. I go deeper into my nod, but then I hear a rattle. It is my father's key in the door, footsteps coming upstairs. I find it hard to breath. I can't catch my breath. That sinking feeling in the pit of my stomach is getting worse. My heart is beating faster. I hear him come in the door, through the dining room, through the kitchen, and into the bathroom and pee. It is so loud, the sound of the urine hitting the water.

I start to worry. I really don't want it to wake up my mama. He pees forever and with each passing moment my level of anxiety jumps tenfold.

"Mama, please don't wake up, mama, please don't wake up," I recite in my mind. Then I think, "Hurry up, hurry up, and hurry up," until he is done. Good, she does not wake up. If she wakes up, she will start a fight with him, curse him out, and strike him again and again and again until he finally gets mad and strikes back, and by then it will be too late.

I don't think about it at the time, something else I will never let enter my consciousness, but my sister is awake. She has to be, she gets to the fights too quick. She and I will never talk about it and throughout childhood our eyes rarely meet, but she is my ally. Decades later I will still have this awesome respect for my sister, because she is the only person I know other than myself who can get knocked down or hit upside the head and come out of unconsciousness fighting. I know how hard that is to do. There is that split moment between consciousness and unconsciousness which seems to be eternal, but it is the most important moment that may decide between life and death, consciousness and unconsciousness, parents or no parents.

I can depend on my sister. There would be many episodes when she or I would be thrown against walls, sinks, stoves, refrigerators, or struck with a blow intended for a parent by a parent when we would experience that stark moment between consciousness and unconsciousness. I learn very quickly that at all costs I must always protect my head. I guess my sister knows that too. I can remember being in the middle in between my parents fighting. My sister was trying to pull my mama away from behind, with her arms wrapped around my mother's waist, and I was pushing my father backward away from my mother. My mother flung my sister off her and my sister was thrown to the floor as her head hit the cabinet at the base of the sink. It was not so much seeing that which bothered me as it was the sound. That sound of the skull crashing against wood is unique, and it would echo throughout my life. That sound made my heart skip a beat and that sinking feeling in the pit of my stomach became more pronounced, and that moment of terror penetrated my heart like a knife through butter. As I watched my sister's body slump down to the floor, for a split second I was torn. Do I stop trying to separate the warring factions, or do I run to help my sister? But no worries, I never stop what I am doing and within seconds my sister is up and in the fight again.

I don't have to worry about fighting tonight though; it seems as if my mother is going to sleep through his arrival. He comes out of the bathroom with that glazed look in his eyes and says, "How you doing, slim?"

I reply, "I am O.K.," but I note to myself, I feel different. His "How you doing, slim?" usually makes me feel good, but there is something different this time. I think it is the glazed look in his eyes, that affects me and the way I feel, although I am pleased that he asked. Somehow it makes me want to do for him.

He asks, "What did you have for dinner tonight?" I reply, "Rice, gravy, fried chicken, and collard greens." He says, "Good," and starts to fumble around in the refrigerator. He's making too much noise and I start to worry. If mama wakes up there will be a fight. She will definitely curse him out and start to strike at him as she constantly does. So I push him out of the way and tell him to sit down. I think he is grateful because he can hardly stand up.

He takes my seat at the kitchen table and I start to warm up his dinner. I can do it quicker but more importantly quieter than he can. He sits there sometimes watching television and sometimes watching me. His head is hung halfway down to the table. Now he is the one nodding halfway between sleep and consciousness. I stare at him. I think that I'm disgusted, but I don't know what to do so I continue to cook. I give him a paper plate and cup. This is very important. If I dirty up more dishes mama will get mad and there might be another fight or, worse yet, she might beat me. It is late and I do not want to get slapped tonight.

He starts to eat and asks me for the hot sauce. I get it out of the cabinet and within a few minutes, he is sleeping. He is sleeping with his face in the food, again. I sit across the table from him and watch. He is such a pretty man, smooth brown skin, curly hair, wonderful hands, and a big black spot on his thumb where he cut off part of his finger with an ax when he was a child. I sit there staring at him. I take my hand and gently rub his forearm and play with the hair. My little boy fingers look so small against his giant muscular forearm, but I am happy to touch him, that he is home, and that he and my mama have not started fighting again. I clean up the pots and pans and put the food back in the refrigerator. I lift his head out of the plate and clean the food off his face with a paper towel. I go to my room and bring back a pillow and put his head on it. I do this very carefully, I don't want him to start snoring; that might wake up mama and there will be another fight. I put a blanket over his shoulders and run my fingers through his hair. I cut off the light and go to bed. I'm tired.

CHAPTER 9

DEFENSELESS CHILD

I was ten years old when we moved into our new house, and it seemed that with my advancing age my mother and I would have more and longer discussions. After dinner I would dry the dishes as she washed. This was usually my time to receive her education speech about how important schooling was and about how an uneducated black man was doomed to a life of despair. Interestingly enough, as the speeches began it was the first year in which any of us actually failed a grade at school. My sister and brother each would repeat their respective grades, fifth and fourth, the next year. Over the course of that year I would be jealous of the attention they received, especially my sister who apparently was very rambunctious in class and could not be dominated either by my parents or by her teachers.

There was a secret hidden part of me that wanted to be like my sister, who had the courage to tell her teachers "kiss my ass," and as the years progressed she would occasionally tell my mama that. Whenever she did, there was an inner part of me that cheered her on, rallied to her cause, and inwardly hoped for her victory. I myself simply suffer in silence. There are times when I hate drying the dishes with my mama. I feel like a prisoner who cannot get away. Her incessant ranting and raving is driving me crazy. I know that she loves me, wants what is best for me but I feel so burdened, so overwhelmed. I soon learned the price of disobedience, and I would be slapped, beaten, called stupid and jackass. Although I had grown considerably since that day on the corner of Howard Street when my daddy refused to pick me up, I was still incapable of defending myself from the stabbing and jabbing of the knife which now twisted at my heart once again. The overwhelming verbal onslaught that was to be heaped upon me that day was simply more than I could bear.

There is some place within my inner world where I retreated that day and where I would reside on many occasions. That world is far removed from my mother and yet, in a strange way, closely attuned to if not even dependent upon her I say that because I know that I have this sixth sense, but sometimes it fails me and all of a sudden I get attacked from behind, slapped upside the head. I see black subtly outlined with these bursting images as I try to wipe away the pain and the sting from my flesh. I learn to fear my mother's wedding rings, which always hurt even more than the rest of her hand.

I think that I cause some of these attacks. I am unsure why. I cannot stop. I think that I loathe the contempt and viciousness which my mama sometimes shows toward me, but I cannot speak or defend myself. It is almost like I don't know how. I defiantly stand there as she strikes me. I refuse to cry, to move, or to show emotion of any kind. She strikes harder, more often and more viciously, but she is asking something of me which I cannot give. She gives up, calls me stupid and jackass, then we go back to finish the dishes.

She continues to talk, sometimes with moments of dead silence. She does not know that I am no longer there. Strange as it may seem, this attack occurred as a response to my utterance of a single phrase, "I didn't ask to be born." I don't know why I said that to my mother that day. I do know that I was tired, but of what I am not sure.

I never would say those words to my mama again, but each time I would taste the blood in my mouth from that beating I would hate her. Although I am unsure, I think I learned to resent that day. My mother was bigger than I and stronger than I, so I kept my mouth shut, but I would find it difficult to forgive her. I would always harbor resentment over that beating.

It is not so much the beating or the cussing that she gives me, but it is the look in her eyes. She stares into my eyes and enters my soul with so much force. She is so strong. I cannot stop her. She races her way past everything I have ever learned to do to protect myself. I sense this fierce, utter brutality and I am unable to stop it. Her eyes say in action what her mouth has said before, "Do what I say or I will kill you." I believe her. It is this belief that strikes terror in my soul. I feel a chill up my spine and I tremble. I do not want to die.

I shut up and do as she demands, but there is a part of me dying in the process. There is this part of me falling away which I cannot stop or hold onto. I have these repeated dreams where I am simply falling, never reaching bottom. I scream and holler but nothing comes out. I reach and stretch for something to hold onto to break my fall or only to slow it, but there is nothing. I continue to fall without end. I continued to dry the dishes that day, but just like in my dreams I could feel myself falling away. That feeling of falling away became a habit, a tradition, an image as to the way I am. I am unable to stop; its hold is too strong.

I think it was about this time when I started to feel guilty. It seems like nothing I do is ever enough. My mama is struggling so hard to feed us and take care of us. She complains about the bills all the time and about how much it costs to take care of us and feed us and clothe us. I feel guilty. I try not to eat, but sometimes I can't stand it and I go pillaging through the refrigerator. She complains that I eat too much and that I cannot possibly be hungry again. I do listen to her, but soon I cannot tell when I am hungry. My stomach growls and rattles but I am not sure what that means. I think it means that I am selfish and don't care about the rest of the family I am ashamed. I despise myself, I hate myself, yet I cannot stop. I see my mama despising me. Sometimes she doesn't say anything, but each time I go to the refrigerator she stares at me out the corner of her eye. I pretend that I don't notice. I wish that I didn't exist.

CHAPTER 10

DADDY FORGOT MY BIRTHDAY

I have been trying to pull my mother back off my father for what seems like forever. She has the big fork she uses to turn the ham she sometimes cooks on Sunday. She is trying to stab him with the fork. My sister tries to separate them, but I can see she is afraid this time. I can see the fear in her eyes. She is afraid of getting stabbed. I don't blame her, I am afraid myself, but I don't know what else to do, so I continue to fight.

Usually my sister and I can break them up, but sometimes they fight so long and hard that we cannot handle them. I try, I really try but they are so big, too strong, and sometimes I get tired. My face is stinging bad from where mama has been slapping me. I feel my body tiring, getting weaker. I hurt all over and I can no longer defend myself. I am afraid of blacking out. I feel so stupid. I try to hold on. I try very hard. I can feel myself sinking into that black hole but I know that I cannot.

I have to hold on. I think that I have already blacked out. I can't tell. She is still hitting me. I lie there. I pray, "God, please help me," but, alas, God doesn't care. I think that I am going to die no matter what I can't stop her from hitting me. I don't remember what happened that night, but I do remember being very happy the next day.

I think that I was happy because I woke up. It was like nothing could go wrong all day because I woke up. It seemed like that happiness lasted forever. I was mighty sore. It seemed like everything on my body hurt, but I didn't care. I took a lot of naps that day. It seemed like I was tired but I am unsure. I just can't remember. I can remember being happy, of that I am certain.

I am unsure why I remember some things from childhood so clearly, so vividly, and other things seem to be veiled in mystery. I can remember my happiness like it was yesterday, but everything else I see through a fog. I do remember my sister staring at me from the doorway. I never thought about it while we were growing up, but I suspect that my sister cares about me. She is a good ally. I will never voice it during childhood but I appreciate her concern.

I think she is worried. She needs me. I will not let her down. I think she knows that as she goes off to play. During our childhood my sister and I, had only one fight, and other than that I am at a loss to even remember harsh or cross words between us. I don't know why this is. All I know is that I could never hurt her. I suspect this is because of all the beatings I have seen her take. It is as if there is a part of me that hurts for her. She is my ally.

Sometimes our household was filled with laughter. Such was the episode of my father losing the family car. He comes home as usual very late. In the morning he admits to my mama that he has lost the car. My mother goes through the roof and cannot believe that he has actually lost a car. I remember my sister standing in front of him in her pink pajamas with braids in her hair. She was shaking her head, looking at him with ridicule, and saying in a much exaggerated tone of voice, "You lost the car, how can you lose a car?" He tells her to go ahead about her business, but under their breath they both are laughing.

He, my mother, and our next door neighbor go to the area where we used to live around the Fifty Bar. Eventually they did find the car that day, but my mama never again would allow him to drive the family car unless she was with him.

My mama gave me a birthday party when I turned eleven years old. I remember being very proud to turn eleven. My mother, my sister and brother and I ate cake and ice cream with a couple of my friends. I was very excited about my new baseball cards. I loved baseball. I remember hoping and waiting for my daddy to show up for the party, but he never did. I guess he was busy or something, but I really missed him.

I can sense that my mother is very angry at him and this worries me. Later that night after my brother and sister went to bed we talked about my daddy. I let her know it was O.K., I really didn't care. It didn't seem to do much good though, she was still very angry. I kind of wanted to go play, but we just sat there. She told me about what a bad daddy he was and about how she never wanted me to grow up and be like him.

As I lay in bed that night I remember being really confused. I was happy, proud, and excited to turn eleven, but I was also confused as to why my daddy did not show up. I wanted to be with him, but I was kind of mad at him too.

I kind of worried about my mama, she stays mad all the time, and I think that I am kind of mad at her too. She talks very bad about my daddy. My daddy did show up a few days later though. We were playing outside when I saw my daddy come walking down the street. When I saw him I got excited. I ran as fast as I could all the way down to the end of the street.

I was happy to see my daddy. I yelled while running, "I had a birthday and I turned eleven years old," as I jumped and flew into him as hard as I could. He looked at me and said, kind of in a questioning tone, 'You had a birthday, well congratulations." We walked back to the house and I grabbed onto him with both arms and I squeezed as tight as I could and held on. I laid my head against him all the way down the street. I don't know why I held onto my daddy so tight that day. I think that I wanted to crawl up into his arms. I don't even know what I wanted to hide from. All I know is that I wanted to hide.

As we walked down the street I closed my eyes, held onto him, and in a way I hid. I held on all the way up the front porch stairs, and when he got to the top he made me let go. I went back to playing with my siblings. Soon, we could hear the yelling and screaming from outside the kitchen window. I remember feeling embarrassed and ashamed as some of the neighborhood kids stared at us. They never said anything, they just stared.

As my sister and I headed inside I can remember feeling tired. Usually I was the first one there to break up their fights, but not this time. It seemed liked the climb up that interior staircase lasted forever that day. It was as if each step carried with it this enormous weight. My sister stopped on the landing where the staircase twisted and she looked down and back as if to say, "You coming?"

Then I took another step. I think that was the hardest step I took throughout childhood. As my sister opened the interior door it was as if the yelling and screaming rushed out at me and gushed over my body, immersing me. It was as if I could hear the sounds of flesh pounding against flesh. I could feel blood splattering my body and the sting of my own flesh burning and tasting my own blood while seeing the fear in the eyes of those I love all at the same time from a thousand fights before.

I think I expected or wanted something from my daddy that day while running toward him as fast as I could. Whatever it was that I wanted, I never got it.

I don't know what it is about childhood that would make each fight so different. Sometimes I could go into the most intense violent situation completely calm and totally collected, and other times I would be crying like a baby. Today would be one of the totally calm and collected days.

As my sister opened the door it was as if the experience submerged me into a new reality. Just like swimming underneath the water at Orchard Beach. I take a huge breath and I hold it as long as I can.

Just like swimming at Orchard Beach my body goes into its mechanical motions, only this time it is without thought or emotion of any kind. It is instinctive. I've played this roll a thousand times before. It does not need any thought anymore I've done it too often. It is a job. It is a job I hate and despise but a job none the less. I go into these rote motions to separate the warring parties.

After it is over I go to the interior staircase. I sit down on the landing where my sister had beckoned for me by stopping and never saying a word. I sit there. I don't think. I don't feel. I just sit there in the corner with my back against the wall with my knees against my chest, holding my legs and staring into nowhere. Before I know it I have sat there for hours. All of a sudden I realize that the sun has dropped and that I have been sitting in the dark. It is time to go to bed. As I climbed those last few steps to enter the house that night I could feel myself falling, just falling away.

That dream that I had so often had where I was falling without stopping was now entering my waking hours. As I slept that night I dreamed once again of falling away while screaming silently. There seems to be a certain type of peace about this dream intermingled with the terror. I think because although I am in it, I also am not. I would be in a corner of my room as if suspended from a ceiling, on the outside of existence, and although I could feel myself, falling I could also watch myself so I knew that I really wasn't there. Regardless, it gave me a certain type of peace and for that I am grateful.

CHAPTER 11

BASEBALL AND LETTING MY PARENTS DOWN

We joined a new church in the neighborhood. It had a Little League team and my brother and I played organized baseball for the first time. I played first base, but sometimes I was the catcher. I like catching the best. My brother pitches but sometimes he plays shortstop and from time to time we both play the outfield. I like the running, the jumping, the throwing, and just using my body.

I don't like hitting a lot. I am not very good at it. I think my daddy is ashamed of the way I hit, and my mother criticizes me all the time. It makes it hard for me to enjoy the game, and although I play, sometimes I wish I didn't have to. I do like my baseball coach, a nice man. He showed me what I was doing wrong, and I did get a lot better at hitting. I go to school with his daughter, and she is very cute. I think she is the prettiest girl in the sixth grade, and she's even smart. I think I have a crush on her, but I am not real sure what that means yet. All I know is that I like her a lot, and whenever I see her I get real nervous.

It is a different type of nervousness, though, than the nervousness I get when my parents fight, but I think that I sometimes get the two confused. She is really pretty, but whenever I am around her I don't know what to say. I can't stop myself from looking at her, although I would die if she knew, so I usually do this out the corner of my eyes.

It is my turn to hit and I think she is watching me. I think I'm supposed to be watching the ball, but I can't. It's like I can feel her eyes on my back. I try very hard to hit the ball, because I want her to like me. I want her to like me a lot. I feel very bad because I just struck out, so I go back to the corner of the bench and I sit by myself with my head down, hoping no one will notice me, but I still can't stop myself from watching her. I don't know what I'm supposed to do, but this feeling is killing me.

Later on I get a hit. I feel a lot better standing there on first base. I know that I'm supposed to be paying attention to the game, but I can't stop myself, so after every pitch I look over to see if she is watching me. She looks cute in her short pants and sneakers. I love her long brown hair and I even like her braces.

I am so afraid. We are all walking back to the cars and she says hello to me and I panic. My mouth gets dry. I cannot swallow or wet my tongue as I try to say hello. I feel like I've messed up because I couldn't say hello. I worried about that all night and turned over a lot in my bed. The next day in school, I see her again and she is still cute. I kind of keep my distance though, but I am still admiring her. I'm admiring her a lot.

The very best baseball game I ever had was one day when my brother was pitching and I was catching. I struck out three times that day, but my last time at bat I hit a grand-slam home run. My brother hit a home run that day too and drove in three runs. We won that game seven to nothing. I was happy. One of the other guys on the team came over and said "The Williams brothers," and that made me feel good.

As we walked back to the car I asked my mother had I done good. She looked at me and asked, "When are you going to learn how to hit?" I felt that sinking feeling in my stomach but it wasn't too bad this time. I think I was getting used to it.

During the ride home that evening my mother kept telling me what I needed to do to be a better hitter to not strike out so much, and I felt bad. I wanted to promise to do better next time, but I just sat there. I had listened to my mama talk about me with the other parents during the baseball game. She says that I am not very tough and that I am not like the other boys and she does not know what to do with me. I feel ashamed that I am not what she wants me to be, and I am constantly embarrassed by this, but I don't know how to be what she wants me to be.

I have let her down. I am unworthy of her time, love, and attention. I am sad and I think that I am something else, but I am unable to tell. I cannot really grasp what is going on with me. All I know is that I am embarrassed by who I am and ashamed of the fact that I exist. I don't really know why I am here; all I ever do is make my mama ashamed all the time. I really want her to love me, but it is almost as if I won't let myself really think about it. So I keep it in the back of my mind, never allowing it to come to the front. This way I don't have to be hurt more than I already am.

One of the best times of my childhood was the baseball game my family went to at Shea Stadium in New York to see the New York Mets, although I liked the Yankees too. This was a lot of fun and I got to eat hot dogs too. We all stood up and sang during the seventh-inning stretch as I stretched my back and arms and just sang, sang, sang. My brother and I studied the players and their stats, and from time to time my daddy hollered at the umpire when he made a mistake.

There is not much I regret in my life when it comes to baseball. I guess the only thing I regret is the promises my daddy made that were never fulfilled. I used to dream of just the two of us, he and I together at the baseball game.

When I lost my father, not knowing whether he was dead or alive somewhere between Georgia and Tennessee, well into my adulthood, there was only one thing that I wanted him to know. I wanted him to know that I waited. If I could say anything to him I think I would say that I waited.

I wanted him to remember when I was a little boy and he would promise to take me to the baseball game, just he and I..

I did not love much as a child, but I did love baseball. I loved watching baseball. I loved playing baseball. I loved talking about baseball. I loved listening to baseball on the radio. I loved thinking about and dreaming about baseball. The only thing that I loved more in the entire world than baseball was my daddy. I knew that I loved him more than I loved baseball.

Maybe that's why I was so excited when he promised to take me to the baseball game. All week long, every day at school, I dreamed about him and me at the baseball game. That Friday night I could hardly sleep because I was so excited that he was going to take me to the baseball game. I tossed and turned all night long, and I went to bed with my baseball, my baseball glove, and my baseball cards. I waited until everybody was sleep and I took my little flashlight and I stared at my baseball heroes who I would see tomorrow.

When I wasn't looking at my baseball cards I was lying there with my New York Yankees baseball cap on and throwing my baseball into the center of my glove. Although Mickey Mantle, Willie Mays, Yogi Bera, Boog Powell were my heroes, none were bigger or greater in my heart than my daddy. He was my real hero. The man I wanted to be like. The man I looked up to. He always was my hero and I guess he still is.

I remember he didn't come home that night. I wasn't worried though. I knew he would be there tomorrow. I got up early the next morning I was excited and I finished my chores early too. Then I got ready because my daddy was going to take me to see my other heroes. I cannot remember a time of more joy, of more excitement, or of more love.

I put on my brand-new blue jeans, which were too long even after mama washed them. I cuffed them two or three times and put on my white high-top Converse sneakers, which I had just washed. I wanted to make my daddy proud. I put on my orange T shirt, the one that said "Chicks" on the front of it; the name of my Little League team. I put on my New York Yankees baseball cap. That was a big decision, whether to wear my Yankees cap or my Little League cap. I got my glove, because I wanted to be ready to catch any fly balls or fouls that might come into the stands were we would be sitting.

I sat on the front porch and I waited for my daddy, because I knew he would be home soon. I dreamed about what a good time we were going to have, and every five minutes I got up and stared down the street, knowing that I would see him any minute. I started waiting about noon. I waited for one hour, two hours, three hours, and I knew the baseball game started about four, but I also knew that I was going to see my daddy any minute and we would get there just in time or maybe just a little bit late.

I dreamed about the good time we would have, the peanuts we would eat, and how we would sing during the seventh-inning stretch. Then it came, four o'clock. I saw my sister staring at me from around the bushes. I knew that she thought daddy was not going to show but she was my little sister and after all what did girls know. This was a guy thing, and I knew that my daddy would not forget me. I knew that we were probably going to a night game and a double header at that; so I waited.

It was around dinnertime when mama came and got me, but I refused to eat. I was not going to fill up on real food when any minute now it was going to be peanuts, soda pop, and cotton candy heaven. I would show them. I'd show them all cause my daddy was going to take me to the baseball game. I still got up every five minutes and stared down the street and any minute I was going to see my daddy, run into his arms and off we would be to the baseball game.

Mama got very angry with me. I could feel her staring at me from the upstairs balcony. She called me stupid and a jackass but it was O.K. - after all she was a girl and she just didn't understand that my daddy would be there any minute. When she came downstairs, she told me to come in, that it was getting dark, but I said no and she slapped me really hard. It hurt a lot but I didn't care because I knew that daddy would be there any minute.

It finally got to be really late, about ten o'clock or something, and she told me that I had to come in. She called me stupid again, and my sister and brother laughed; but it was O.K., brothers and sisters just don't understand, and, after all, I was the oldest and I could take it.

My mama made me come in. I had to, because I didn't want to get slapped again, but I went to the second-story balcony and I waited for daddy. Every five minutes I got up and I leaned over as far as I could and stared down the street to see if I could see my daddy. I sat in an old lawn chair on the balcony and listened to the replay of the baseball game on my little pocket radio while throwing my ball into my glove.

I figured we were probably going to a Sunday game. I slept on the balcony all night that night. I guess somehow I just fell asleep. I remember waking up a little after five A.M. and couldn't wait for the sun to come up so I could go out on the front porch and wait for daddy. That episode would replay itself many times throughout my childhood, but I always waited. I never doubted. I never worried. I just waited.

I would be called dumb, stupid, and jackass many times over the years while I waited, and that was O.K. It was even O.K. when I was laughed at or when mama would slap me for, as she would say, "being so stupid." She never understood. My brother was too young. My sister was a girl and mama, well you know, mamas are just mamas.

They never understood that I loved my daddy, and that I would have waited for him forever. It has been about three decades or so since the first time I waited for my daddy. Still to this day there is a part of that little boy, sitting there on that porch still waiting, never doubting and never worried.

CHAPTER 12

I LOOK LIKE MY DADDY - I APOLOGIZE

Throughout childhood I always feel like I am my mama's favorite. She talks with me longer and more intensely than with any others and I have this overwhelming feeling that I certainly belong to her. Over the years I become a good listener. I learn to pick out the parts of her ranting and raving that are useful and we discuss these into late hours. Although I have the sensation of being a prisoner sometimes during these conversations, I feel like I have an obligation to be there. If I do a good job and can help her figure out my daddy's drinking, then she will love me.

Sometimes when she is angry at my daddy I can talk her out of her anger before my daddy gets home, and that is very useful. I think that I want someone to talk to me, especially at times when my daddy disappears. Sometimes she tells me of all the things she wants me to be or do, and she tells me that she wants me to be the best at whatever I do. She is always pushing me to be the best at whatever I do. If I get a C+ at school, then she wants me to get a B+, then she wants me to get an A+. She pushes me like this almost every day. She wants me to do well, but I get nervous and upset from all the pressure. I think that I am afraid that I won't live up to her wishes, because I never do.

I know she does this because she wants what's best for me. Sometimes I overhear her bragging to her friends about what a good child I am and about how I never cause trouble. She likes the fact that I am quiet and spend a lot of time by myself.

My sister, on the other hand, is always in trouble. Sometimes she gets spankings because she won't shut up. Sometimes I see them coming and I feel for her and I am afraid for her, but she never shuts up. The weird thing, though, is that is what I like best about my sister; the fact that she won't shut up. She says a lot of things to my mama that I would never say, but she constantly has welt marks on her skin from the beatings. It is the price we pay for saying certain things.

Somehow when she says these things it makes me feel better on the inside, but I think it bothers me seeing all the welt marks she suffers through. Sometimes I just stare at my sister when she doesn't know that I am looking. I think that I get taken over or amazed by all the welt marks. It is how I can always tell whenever she has been beat up with the electrical cord. I don't know what it is about my sister, but there is a lot about her that I would like to be like.

My brother is the cutest of the three of us and he is the baby. He makes everyone laugh all the time and is always cracking jokes. He doesn't seem to hang around as much as my sister and I, in fact I don't know where he is most of the time. When we were younger and we would all be riding in the car, sometimes he would sit on my lap. I think he liked the air blowing on him. Now that he has gotten bigger, he always sits in the middle in between my sister and I.

He loses his lunch money a lot at school or loses his lunch, my sister or I have to buy him lunch or give him part of our lunch. Sometimes we just give him money, but I am not sure what he does with his money. He is the only one of the three of us who can get away with saying some things to mama without getting a beating. No matter what he says, they always think it's funny. Sometimes he says things that would get me beat up with the electrical cord or would probably get my sister killed. I can't understand it. I guess he really is her baby. They do look a lot alike. Well, anyway, he is my brother and I love him a lot.

My mama says that she is friends with her children and that it is not just a parent-child relationship. She feels as if we are growing up together. She says that a lot. She was always happy that she had her children early and got that out of the way, as she would say. My mama turned nineteen two days before I was born, and none of us kids are a complete year older than the other. We are all eleven months older than the next one. I think that it made my mama feel good to know that she was growing up with her kids.

Sometimes my relationship with my mama is very intense. I think she works with me more than she works with the others. Although I think she beats my sister more and gives my brother more candy, money, or anything else that is good.

I am afraid of my mama. I never can tell when she is getting ready to explode. Sometimes right in the middle of conversations she stops and says, "You look just like your father." She would say this tenderly and it would make me feel good. At other times she stops and says, "You look just like your father," and I would feel like I had done something wrong. Sometimes I think she hates that I look like my daddy. It is at these times that I am the most afraid. It is at these times when I most want to hide and it is at these times when I am the most confused.

I think that I am confused because after she says, "You look just like your father," I cannot tell if I will receive a loving caress of her hand across my head or a fist thrown against my head. There are times during my childhood that I jump or cover up with fear of my mama for no reason at all.

The first day my daddy leaves is always the most dangerous. I can never tell what will happen. Sometimes we go right into our long discussions about my daddy's drinking, but at other times she is angry and completely consumed with rage. At these times I get beaten the worst. As if it were yesterday I can still feel the sting of that electrical cord as I would dance and jump to try to avoid the next blow. She grabs my hand with hers so that I cannot get away I scream, holler, and crawl across the floor to get away.

Sometimes I go into the bathroom and soak my washcloth with water and try to tend to the welt marks which often ooze with blood.

I try to figure out what it is that I did or said wrong. I am at a loss. I sit on top of the toilet or on the bathroom floor with the bathroom door shut afraid to come outside. I try to sense what is going on outside I think I spend a lot of time in the bathroom. Sometimes I don't think I know what to do. There are times when I long to be close to my mama and I lay my head on her shoulder or try to touch my head to hers, but at other times I am terrified just to be in the same room. Often I cannot tell one time from another. All I know is that I love my mama very much, but sometimes my love is filled with anger and sometimes with tenderness and sometimes with resentment.

Most of the time I try to keep a good distance away from her. Sometimes I loathe being within arms reach, but I am not quite sure why. "If it wasn't for you kids" is my most often heard phrase of childhood. It is followed with an entire range of other sayings. "If it wasn't for you kids" I would have a better car, wear better clothes, could afford to go out but the beginning is always the same: "If it wasn't for you kids."

There are times when I think about running away from home, and sometimes the thought of killing myself races across my mind. My mama says that I am "not all there"; but I try not to think about it for long and sometimes I am afraid she might be right. I know that I am not like everyone else, especially the other kids I hang around with, but I don't know what to do. I feel trapped and I cannot get away. I am sad, and when I go to bed at night and try to go to sleep I cannot. There is so much to figure out, so much to do, so much to be afraid of, and I worry a lot, but it is as if I cannot stop. I guess the crazy part is that most of the time I am not real sure what I am even worried about.

Sometimes I catch myself crying right in the middle of walking home from school, or sometimes when I am playing baseball all of a sudden I just feel like crying. Most of the time I hide it pretty well though. I don't want anybody to worry about me, because I have a lot to do and a lot of people depending on me. When I go to bed at night though, I cannot help myself. There I lie alone in the dark.

It is especially bad after my parents finish fighting. I just lie there and cry, quietly, with the covers pulled up over my head. Before I know it, it is over. The morning has come and I start another day.

CHAPTER 13

LEARNING ABOUT SEX

I don't know when I first realized my parents weren't having sex. I may have been about eleven or twelve years old.

My mother had gone through my father's trousers and found a rubber. My father then came home drunk. He goes straight into the bedroom and within minutes they are arguing. My mama asks, "Who are you using this with?" Then she says, "You're certainly not using it with me." Her tone of voice scares me. Then I hear a slap. That sound that skin makes when a hand is brought squarely against it. As I lay in the bed, in darkness I knew she had slapped him. I then hear him say in a low tone of voice, "Why did you do that?" I get that sinking feeling in the pit of my stomach. I don't want to get up. She is hitting him repeatedly; I hear the sound of flesh pounding against flesh. I hear him say, "Alice, stop, Alice, stop it!" Apparently she will not, but I lie in bed determined to weather the storm.

Then I hear footsteps coming out of their bedroom heading toward the kitchen. I know my mama is going after a knife. I jump out of bed just in time to hear the rattle of the silverware drawer. I stand there in the doorway between my mama and my daddy so she cannot get to him. She tells me to move, but I stand still. I shout, "Stop, please stop!" but she will not and she runs me over to get at my daddy. I am knocked down because she is bigger than me, but my sister grabs her from behind, and my sister and I wrestle my mama to the floor and remove the knife from her hands. I quickly run to the living room and hide the knife under the couch as she is screaming at my daddy, "I'll kill you, I'll kill you!" I get back just in time, because now my mama is going after the big fork that she uses to turn the ham on Sunday, and she is trying to stab my daddy.

My sister is pulling my mama from behind, begging and pleading, "No, no, no." as she is trying with all her might to keep my mama away from my daddy. As they wrestle and tug, I stand there for a moment. I don't know if I'm tired or afraid, but for whatever reason I cannot move. Suddenly I recover and I go to help my sister restrain my mama. My sister and I are crying by now.

We will not let my mama move. We are both holding her as tight as we can and my mama is desperately trying to break out as we beg and plead, "Stop, stop, please stop!" It is as if she cannot hear us and we three continue to fight, wrestle, and struggle until we are all tired and can no longer move. She promises to stop if we let go, but we continue to ask four or five times the same question one after the other. "Are you going to kill him?" "Do you promise you will not kill him"? We cannot stop asking the same question repeatedly. I am afraid to let go. I am afraid she will kill him.

As I look back on that moment I suspect that I just wanted to hold onto my mama. It is the only time I ever held onto my mama.

When my sister and I finally let go, she promises that they will only talk. Now she and my daddy are arguing, but my sister and I will not leave. We are afraid. My sister and I watch in horror and disbelief as they argue. We cannot move. It is as if we are stone, each frozen in this place that we do not want to be. My father left the house that night, but I could not go back to sleep. Soon it is morning and I watch the light slowly creep into my bedroom and I get ready to start my day to go to school.

As I think back to last night, I do not understand why my mama picks a fight with someone who is bigger and stronger than any of us. It is almost as if she can't leave him alone, and it makes me angry. Sometimes he comes home drunk and falls asleep at the kitchen table with his face in the food sound asleep. She comes into the kitchen and stares at him with a consuming look of rage and contempt that I have seen so often.

Sometimes she goes back to bed and leaves him alone. Often she attacks him as he sleeps. I guess what makes me mad is that she argues so hard with someone who is drunk. No matter how hard I try, I just can't make sense of it or figure it out. I think I just resent the fact that she never leaves him alone. I think that I am just tired of the fighting. I don't care what has to be done or what doesn't get done, I just don't care. I just want the fighting to stop.

There are times that I lie in bed waiting for my daddy to come home. I am nervous, scared, and unable to sleep. I know that my mama is also lying in bed awake, waiting for him to come home.

My father starts leaving the house more and more whenever she is consumed with rage. He says he is trying to avoid the fighting, that is the right thing for a man to do. Sometimes he is too drunk to leave. I feel like my mama is running my daddy off, and that makes me mad. I do not like her for that, because sometimes when he leaves, he does not come back for days or weeks at a time. I want him to be here so someone will grab me by the top of my head and say, "How you doing, Slim?" I don't care who does it but I want someone to know I am alive. No one knows that I am here.

I think that my mama wants me to hate my daddy, and I would if I could just to make her happy, but it is hard. I love both of them, and I can hardly ever choose one over the other. Sometimes they have these low muffled arguments late at night when we are all in bed. I hear my mama say, "Don't ever wake me up for that again!" I guess she got her way, because the low muffled arguments have stopped, but the fights continue and are becoming worse.

I wonder why they ever got married. I know they met at a party in Harlem. My father was living in New York and my mother was living with her mama in New Jersey. My godfather, Nathaniel, introduced them, but I sure don't see what they saw in each other that would make them want to be married. My mama is very smart. No one can outthink her, and she is strong-willed and determined. People love her and follow her. She has been president of our church's Rosary Society for as long as I can remember, and she speaks really well.

My daddy is kind of slow. I don't think he ever thinks about anything. He is extremely quiet and rarely talks about anything, except maybe to tell a joke. When he is drunk he is even quieter and usually goes to sleep. He can barely read or write, and it takes him forever just to sign his name. When he is sober, it seems that he is always sad. Sometimes I watch him while he is sitting at the table just staring out into space with this "thousand-yard stare." I don't quite know where he is during those times, but I don't think it is a good place. I know why my daddy would want to be married to my mama. She is smart and can hold things together.

I think when I was younger daddy did love her. Sometimes he would grab her and hold onto her. I remember he did that in the supermarket and kissed her. She got angry and told him never to do that in public again. Sometimes he is passionate that way, but, regardless, she got her way and he hardly notices her anymore. What confuses me is why she would ever want to be married to him. She hates him most of the time. He can be fun sometimes, or at least more fun than she is, but somehow it doesn't seem to make sense.

One day while reading the dates on the inside of our family Bible, all of a sudden I realize that my parents were married in May and I was born in October. I asked my mama about this and she replied in a stern voice, "I was married when all my children were born." I went back to reading the Bible and I remembered they taught us in school that it takes nine months for a baby to be born. I go back to my mama and ask her about this. Then she swings back and slaps me as hard as she can. The force of the blow causes me to bend over, but as I am trying to rise she catches me with a fist to the head and I am bent over again. I feel her fists pounding my back, head, and shoulders as the pain shoots through my body. I am unable to handle the barrage of swinging fists, and I run as fast as I can. I run back to the living room crying. I don't think I cried because of the pain that day. I cried because I didn't see this one coming, and my sixth sense failed me.

I pass my brother as I stumble back into the living room. He has this look in his eyes that says, "I can't believe you asked her that." It is almost as if he knew I was going to get it. I feel very stupid.

I think in my family there were always things that we weren't suppose to talk about, but somehow I had never picked up on the fact that my birth was one of those things. I think that I am stupid and I feel trapped. I feel trapped because I want to know about my birth.

CHAPTER 14

RUNAWAY CHILDHOOD

My mother tried to stab my sister with a butcher knife the other day. I am not sure why. My sister is quick and was able to get out of the way, but my mama did catch her upside the head with a cast-iron frying pan and she ran away from home. They went out looking for her, but they were unable to find her. In a way I am happy for my sister, but I am also afraid for her and hope that she is O.K.

My sister is afraid of my mama. I don't really blame her, I am afraid of mama myself, but she doesn't beat me up as much as she does my sister. I sometimes think that my mama does not like my sister very much. I don't know why, it is just a feeling I have.

I cannot seem to grasp onto my sister the way I can my father. My sister is somewhat harder to get hold of. It feels as if she bounces back and forth between anger and fear, anger and fear. I really wish that I could help my sister, but I don't know how. Sometimes I am afraid for her, especially when my mama is beating her.

When they finally find my sister, she goes to live with my aunt and uncle for a while. I cannot stand my sister being away from me. A part of me needs to watch out for her. All I know is I feel as if I am about to explode when she is not here. I lied to my mama one night and went to see my sister. I am afraid, because if I get caught my mama will be angry with me. I don't want to get kicked out of the house like my sister. I lay my eyes on my sister and I am relieved because it is the first time I have seen her since she ran away, but I also feel like I am getting ready to jump out of my skin. I can't stand still, and whatever it is that I am feeling, I want to run away from it.

My aunt leaves her and me alone in the living room. As I talk to my sister I give her all my money. I try to ask her what is wrong and what happened but she refuses to talk. As I talk I am in a panic and I want to run away from and hold onto her at the same time. As I look back on that day I can only see it through my own tears, and I was hurt, angry, confused, frustrated, lonely, shocked, and in terror.

My sister sat there calm and quiet. She assures me that she is all right and that there is nothing to worry about. She will not share with me why she has run away and she does not cry I want to be strong and I want to help her, but I don't seem to be able to stop crying. At first she even refuses to accept the money that I want to give her until I force her to keep it. She tries to reassure and comfort me, her older brother who had come to help her.

As I walked back home through the cold New Jersey streets with tears rolling down my face, I knew that I was hurting for her more than she could hurt for herself. I think that my sister was the one who bled for the family. No matter what our woes, hurts, ills, or burdens, I think my sister was the one who bled for the family. I think my sister was the most sensitive, the most gifted, and the most fragile of the children, and I think it is the one who is the most gifted who is hurt the most.

Sometimes I still see this hurt, fragile little girl whom I want to cradle and cuddle and would have fought the world to protect. As I look back on the days of my sister running away from home, I am unsure if my sister ran away, or if our childhood somehow ran away from us.

CHAPTER 15

GROWING WEAKER IN CHILDHOOD

I started to feel smaller and weaker. I don't know how this happened or even when it happened, but more and more I felt more afraid.

Sometimes I get beaten with the electrical cord. There is no beating that I fear more. You would think there would be moments in my life when I actually learned something. Moments when I say, "I'll never do that again," but there are not, not one. Somehow whenever I get beaten with the electrical cord, there is nothing but anger. I am angry at being small and weak. I am angry at being unable to control what I want. I am angry at my parents.

I don't know why I get so angry at my parents whenever they beat us with the electrical cord. Regardless, I do know that as I grow up I feel afraid. Like the day I watched my parents beat my sister with the electrical cord. I watch my mother tell my father that my sister needs to be beaten as they all stand there in the dining room arguing about whatever it is that she has done. I think it had something to do with a boy.

My sister learned to like boys when she was young. I don't know if she liked the boys or if she just wanted to run away to get loved. I know it doesn't make much sense but it is the feeling I have. From the very first beating I ever watch my sister get I know there is a part of her that no one can get to. I think that part is afraid. I could feel that part the day I went to visit her at my Aunt's house as I held her and drew her close to me before I left, but during our entire childhood we never once mention it. I think we are too afraid to mention it and I don't even mention it to myself. Although I have seen my sister get beaten for what seems like a thousand times, this beating upsets me. You would think that I would be used to it by now. My sister hops, skips, jumps, and tries to run away from my daddy as he holds onto her. She cannot get away as he raises his arm again and again to strike her, each time flinging back as far as he can in order to hurt her, which he does.

My mother is encouraging and directing him, saying in the background as he continues to strike her, "Maybe this will teach you."

I am angry at my mama but I am angrier at my daddy. He never will stand up to my mama, though. Finally, my sister's body goes limp. She no longer jumps or skips or tries to run away, she lies there and takes what she has coming. She whimpers now and then like a dog missing its owner. This is the worst part of a beating. We no longer struggle, but simply accept the will of our parents'. It is almost like I cease to exist at that point, I disappear. I can never win, no matter how hard I struggle. No matter how hard I fight. No matter how hard I try to run away. I will always be beaten into submission.

There is a point in beatings where I can no longer feel pain. The pain starts to run on and on, one blow running into another until I no longer distinguish one blow from the other. Past that point everything becomes a blur and I am unable to think any longer. It is like hitting a dead man - the body moves, it reacts to the force of the blow, but there is no longer any pain. The muscles, nerves, and fibers simply quit. They give up, much like I do submitting to a stronger, more powerful force. I know that my sister reaches this point as she lies there on the dining room floor whimpering as the tears roll down her face.

A part of me wants to save my sister. I want to knock down my daddy and tell my mother to shut up, but I do not. I stand there in the doorway between the dining room and the kitchen and watch them beat my sister until her will is no longer there. I stand there paralyzed, unable to say or do anything to act on her behalf, although I want to with all my heart.

I feel small, like I am three feet tall, and as they continue to beat her I shrink and shrink until I am almost not there. I don't know if I am afraid that they are going to kill my sister or that I am going to disappear.

I try to move but I cannot, and that scares me more. I try harder and harder but I cannot move. I am afraid and I don't know what to do. I can't breathe and I am dying on the inside. I want to move, but they will kill me if I do, so I find a place on the inside and I hide, I don't move. I don't say anything, and I try as hard as I can to just disappear, but they beat her mercilessly and I cannot get away. I cannot leave my sister - they will kill her if I do, but I feel like I am dying. So I stand there, still, motionless, and paralyzed with fear.

After it is over, I stand there in that doorway. I want to move, but I cannot. I try very hard, but I cannot move. I try to cry out, "Help, help, please somebody help!" but I cannot open my mouth. The tears are rolling down my face, but I cannot move and I cannot ask for help. It is just like the dreams I have where I cry out for help and nothing comes out, only worse. I am trapped and a prisoner in my own body.

My sister takes her shirt off as she is sitting there on the dining room chair bent over at the waist with her hands wrapped around herself trying to reach the welts and cuts, which now line her back. I watch the blood ooze out of each, slowly, and with each drop I lose a part of myself that I cannot recover. I watch my mama take a cotton ball and, with a bottle of alcohol, drench the cuts trying to stop the bleeding as my sister cries out in pain. I don't know which hurts her more, the beating or the healing.

CHAPTER 16

BEING FLUNG INTO WALLS

I don't know when the police first started coming to our house, but they came a lot. One of the things I hate most is to call the police when my sister and I are unable to stop my parents from fighting. Sometimes my mama makes the decision for me and demands that I call the police right in the middle of their fighting. Then at other times I decide on my own that things have gotten out of hand and my sister and I can no longer handle them and I will call the police on my own usually when I get scared for my life.

Sometimes the police never show up. My mama says it is because of the neighborhood we live in, but I never do believe that. I think they do not show up because I am a kid. No matter what I do, I can never get anyone's attention.

I can remember so vividly my sister and I trying to break them up and being too small to do so. She and I are flung into more walls, sinks, chairs, and refrigerators than I care to remember. It is a bad thing being thrown or flung away. It is hard to describe the feeling, trying so hard and then just being thrown away. It is almost like being told I am nothing; I never do like the way that feels. I think I resent it. After all, it is their fight. I want to be outside playing with my friends and then they just throw me away like I am nothing. Sometimes when I hit the wall and slump to the floor, there is a part of me that wants to stay there, but I never do. I always get right back up and into the fight. I think I can do this because there is a part of me that doesn't believe it even as it is happening.

I remember my mama flinging me into the refrigerator one day as I was trying to stop her from beating up my sister. Her hand is so hard and strong wrapped around my arm. I resent it. On the inside, I scream and scream at the top of my lungs, "Let me go, get your hands off of me!" On the outside, I remain silent. The resentment is soon replaced by fear, though it may be only for a split second. That second between when I realize I am being flung and fearing what it is that I am about to crash into. That second is the worst when I realize I am about to be hurt and accept that there is nothing I can do about it. I think that moment is worse than the crashing into the wall or refrigerator itself. I don't know why, it just is. I don't think that I would mind getting beat up on if somehow I could avoid that split second of knowing that I am going to be struck and actually being struck. Sometimes I think that I just pretend that it isn't happening.

Maybe that's why when the police show up to break things up, sometimes they just turn around and leave. Sometimes they take my daddy out in handcuffs, though, and they take him downtown. It is a weird feeling watching my daddy sitting in a police car handcuffed. Although the police sometimes come and sometimes they don't, they do come enough that I get to recognize some of the officers.

Somehow, this is kind of embarrassing. I wish they would put new officers on the beat so I would not have to see the same faces. I am supposed to take care of my parents, and each time I have to call the police it is a sign that I am not doing a good job.

77

I remember the police taking my daddy out of the house. I run around the officers to look at my daddy. It is at these times when he is most likely not to show up for weeks or months at a time. As I circle around, a strange thing happens. I think the officer is a little leery of me, afraid that I might grab his gun or something. I had pleaded with this officer in the past, "Please don't take my daddy away from me!" Then all of a sudden our eyes meet. It is like I am locked into his eyes. I know that no one ever really knows what another person is thinking, but I become lost in the eyes of this police officer. Suddenly I am the object of someone's caring. I don't think that I have ever had a feeling like that before, it is so strong, so powerful! I do not know this man and he does not know me, but I think there is a part of him that wants to take me away.

I remember that feeling because of that one moment. That moment when I felt like that police officer wanted to take me away. I don't know where he wants to take me or what he wants to do with me, but I think there is a part of me that wants to go. It doesn't make a difference where he wants to take me or what he wants to do with me, if he asks, I will go. It is a strange feeling and it scares me, but I don't know why. Maybe it scared me because for the first time in my life it made me question. Maybe I am in a situation that would elicit caring? I had never thought of myself that way before.

That moment was fleeting, because after they left, I became filled with resentment. As I watched the police car pull away with my daddy in the back seat, I cannot understand why or how my mama can have my daddy taken away when she is the one who always starts the fights.

There is this part inside of me that sometimes speaks to me about what is going on. I think that look between that policeman and me meant so much to me that day because in a way I wanted to go with him. Maybe, they should have taken me away instead of my daddy?

CHAPTER 17

TRYING TO FEEL

I spend more and more time away from home. I don't know why, I just do. I feel more comfortable in the streets than I do at home. My father starts staying away for longer periods also, until it gets to the point that we hardly expect to see him on Fridays. This may be good since the more he is away the less they fight.

My parents go to court on several occasions concerning my father's paycheck. My mama says he never does bring his paycheck home to feed his family.

I don't know a lot about this court thing. They never take me to court with them. I do know that queasy feeling in my stomach gets bigger each time they go to court. I think I am afraid; if my parents break up, who will be here to take care of us kids. I am afraid if they break up, but I am afraid if they stay together. I know kids whose parents have broken up, and sometimes the kids are separated, with each kid going to a different aunt or uncle. I don't want that to happen in my family.

I never made any decisions during childhood about whether my parents should stay together. I just didn't know what was best. I did know, regardless of what happened between my parents, I did not want my sister and brother to be taken away from me. I think that I worry about this more than I worry about anything else. They are so young and I don't know who will take care of them. I know that I would miss them, even though they sometimes get on my nerves.

I know that my oldest uncle and aunt had taken a cousin to live with them for a while. My other uncle never would let them adopt him, though, so they finally gave him back. I have a feeling they would love to have my sister or brother but probably not all three of us, because that would be too much.

I don't know who I would like to live with if things come to that, but I do know I want the three of us to be together. After my parents go to court, my mother tells me they have garnished my daddy's paycheck. I am not exactly sure what that means and I am afraid to ask. Although I am not real sure what this is all about or what it means, I feel sure that it isn't good.

My daddy doesn't come home until a few weeks later, but they don't fight this time. I overhear him ask, "Did you get your money?" She says, "Yes," and they go ahead about their business.

I learned later on that part of my daddy's paycheck went to the court and then I think the court mailed my mama the money. My daddy works for a textile company down on Tischner Street. He is a factory foreman or something and he has to open up the building every day. My mama tells him all the time how he needs a job with benefits, but my daddy never listens. She does not like the fact that his boss gives him the keys to the building and makes him open up the plant every day. I think my daddy likes that part of his job, though, and is very proud of it. No matter what time my daddy comes home or how drunk he is, he is always up early to open up the plant. He says, "If there is a penny on the street, I'll find it because I'm the first one up."

I don't think my daddy is supposed to be living here. I think it has something to do with the courts and his garnishment. He kind of lives here and kind of lives other places too. He's usually here three or four days a week and then gone for two or three days. Sometimes he stays away for weeks.

Often I miss him when he is gone, so I get on the bus and go down to Howard Street to the Fifty Bar to track him down. Sometimes I find him right away but often I have to really look. A lot of the folks at the Fifty Bar know me, so when I walk in they say, "Hey, you're Pete's boy, aren't you?" I say yes and ask them have they seen my daddy. Sometimes he is shooting craps in the alley way behind the bar or sometimes I walk through the neighborhood until I find him.

When I am not in school, I will sometimes go to his job during the day. He introduces me to all the people he works with and they all say how much I look like him. I think he is very proud of me. It is something about the way he looks at me. I don't know what to say.

He has that sad look in his eyes. Mama is so angry when he is not around. I try to make her happy but I cannot. I'm afraid that if he stays away too long mama will start to beat up on me again.

I don't say anything, though. I don't even really let it enter my mind, but I am afraid of something. He asks, "So how you doing, Slim?" I say, "Fine," and he says, "Well, that's good."

He tells his boss that he is going to take a break and he and I walk out to the front of the building. It is cold; I zip up my coat and put on my gloves. He puts on his jacket and puts the collar up as I watch his breath in the cold afternoon air.

We don't say much. We just stand there. He asks me about Yvonne, then about Peter. Then he says, "Is your mother doing O.K.?" I say, "Yeah, she's O.K.", then we stand there some more. We just kind of stand there not saying anything, just kind of looking around, and occasionally looking at each other. He tells me that he has to go back to work and I say, "O.K."

I watch him as he walks back into the building and watch the door close behind him. I stand there for just a minute. I don't know why, I just do. I put my hands in my pockets and my hood on my head as I walk away trying to figure out what to do next. I cross the street on my way to the bus stop, but before I round the corner, I stare at that building he works in. I lean against the wall and stare at it for a long time. I cannot stop myself. I do not want to leave.

As I am riding home, all kinds of thoughts go through my head. I sometimes relive the fights between my mama and daddy. I can be anywhere and all of a sudden I'll hear the shouting and screaming all over again. That sinking feeling in the pit of my stomach will start and I'll get nervous. I try to stop but I cannot. I don't know what's wrong but I know that I have to get home. I don't want my mama to know that I went to see my daddy. It will upset her and I might get in trouble. She gets angry with me because she says she can't understand why I love him. She talks to me about that a lot. I don't say anything. I'm afraid to say anything, but she says she can tell. I think she wants me to love her more than I love him but I don't. I don't even know why I love him, I just do.

She says that I'm stupid and need to get some sense. Sometimes I feel guilty because I don't feel the way she wants me to.

CHAPTER 18

TERROR OF CLOSENESS IN CHILDHOOD

I plan to leave home as soon as I can. I hate it here. My mama says she can't wait until I'm eighteen and leave her alone. I can't wait until I'm eighteen too, to leave her alone; on this we agree.

"All I want is one minute of peace and quiet," my mama says all the time. She says that we children get on her nerves and she wishes that we would just disappear. She used to say that she wished we would just run away, until my sister did. She says that she'll be glad when we get grown and leave the house. Sometimes I feel sorry for her when she says, "All I want is one minute of peace and quiet." I know what that feels like.

I know one time I asked her, "Why did you have children?" This made her mad and I got slapped. It just seems as if she is angry all the time but I, I can never get angry. If she even suspects that I am angry, then I get slapped or beat up with the electrical cord. She'll ask me, "What is your lip poked out for, what's wrong with you?" When I am asked this it scares me, because if I tell her, I am likely to get beaten. When I was younger I used to tell her why I was angry or what was wrong.

After a few beatings with the electrical cord I've learned to keep my mouth shut. I never tell her anything anymore. I figure it out on my own. It just is the safest thing to do.

I can remember during more than one beating, she would say, "You think you're mad now, wait until I get through with you." Or sometimes she would say, "I don't care if you are mad, you have your whole life to get glad." Then she tells me how her mother used to say that to her when she was a little girl.

This was when I was younger, though. I hardly get angry at anything anymore. It's just too dangerous. If I even think that I'm going to get mad, I take myself to my room or leave the house until it is over. I think this is what my father did when it looked like they were going to get into a fight and he left the house. He told me that this is the right thing for a man to do.

So, just like my daddy, whenever I think that I am going to get mad, I just leave. My daddy is a good example; he hardly ever gets mad, even when my mother is beating him from head to toe. He just takes it, and never says a word. When I look at the bruises and scars on his body I feel better about my own bruises, welts, and cuts.

I think the fact that he hardly ever gets mad makes my mama even madder, though. She tries to make him angry. He comes home drunk as usual, eats, and then falls asleep. She'll come into the room and start arguing with him and hitting him. She'll strike him and strike him while standing right there next to him and he says, "Alice, stop!" Then a second time he says, "Alice, stop!" Then he'll get up and walk into the next room. She follows him and strikes him harder as he says, "Alice, I don't want to fight with you," but she continues and continues until he finally loses his temper and strikes her back.

This makes me angrier than anything else that goes on in our house. It's almost as if she wants him to hit her. I can't understand it, and it scares me and makes me nervous. Then, when they start fighting, my sister and I have to break them up. Sometimes he does leave. Sometimes he does not come back for days or weeks.

Sometimes he is too drunk to leave and he just sits or stands there as my mama whales away at him. This makes my mama even angrier when he refuses to hit her back. When he gets angry, he'll finally let her have one. Then it's almost as if my mama gets what she wants and she is O.K. with this.

They are standing there shouting and hollering at each other and both of them are throwing punches, but it is almost as if somehow this pleases her. At times when he does leave the house and doesn't hit her, she is disappointed. She walks around talking to herself, ranting and raving about how he is a drunk and about how he is no good. She does this for days sometimes.

This is always a difficult time for me. I don't know what is the best thing to do is. I know that if I can get her calmed down then everything will be O.K., but I am afraid.

I don't know why she beats me when he leaves, but I do know that whenever I hear, "You look just like your father," that I better run and run quick.

She doesn't beat me all the time, though, but it is at these times when I am most likely to hear about how dumb and stupid I am or about something I have not quite done well. Usually when he is not around, I just try to be very quiet and not get on her nerves. If he stays away long enough, it is almost as if she and I become best friends. We talk and I lay my head on her shoulder or we just tell jokes and then everything is fine.

Sometimes we get to be so close that when my daddy comes home I am somehow disappointed. When he comes home, then I cease to exist. We go from being best friends to her hardly even noticing that I exist. I don't like this and my daddy and I fight for her attention.

My daddy never gets angry with me the way my mama does, but somehow when we are both trying to get her attention, I don't think he likes me very much. He never says anything. It is just a feeling that I have.

I back away and don't say anything; I know that he'll leave again soon. Then I'll have her all to myself and I can wait.

Often I wish that he would leave forever but then I feel guilty. I would bet, though, she sometimes wishes he would leave forever, too. Sometimes I lay my head on my mother's shoulder and I feel wonderful, but sometimes she touches me and I am consumed with horror. She buys me these new swimming trunks and tells me to try them on. I am excited because my siblings and I go swimming almost every day all summer long. She likes one pair, but she tells me I am too big to wear the other pair. She pinches me on the butt as she tells me this, and I know that it is only a pinch, but I feel weird when she tells me this. It is like being happy, excited, and scared all at the same time. I don't say anything, I just feel weird.

I think that my mama likes it that she and I are so close, but sometimes I just don't know how to handle it. I am taking a bath and she just walks into the bathroom without saying a word. I am sitting in the tub and I try to cover myself. She lifts her dress, pulls down her drawers and proceeds to pee. While looking at me, she says, "What's wrong with you?" I don't answer, but I feel as if she is looking straight through me. She has this way of entering me, straight into my soul.

It is as if my mind, my heart, my soul, they all belong to her, and I feel hollow on the inside. She forces her way past everything I have ever learned to do to protect myself, but this time not with force, more with tenderness and maybe the threat of force. It is as if she possesses me. She tells me to take my bath, as my thoughts turn to my father. He is sitting right outside in the kitchen watching television, but it is as if he doesn't care.

A part of me wants to cry out for him. I feel invaded, useless, worthless, and I try to shrink, to disappear, vanish right there on the inside as I continue to wash my arms and the rest of my body.

The sound of her peeing is so loud and it washes over me and I cannot get away. I find myself confused and struck with terror as she proceeds to talk, but on the inside I am screaming, "Get away from me, and leave me alone." I think to myself, "Run." I don't think anything else, just "run." So I leave, I am in the corner of the ceiling watching myself from above. As the water drains out of the tub, I am going down the drain. I see myself going down the drain, but then I see up from down inside the drain too. I am screaming from inside the drain but I am also reaching down inside the drain desperately trying to save myself in a battle that I am losing. I watch all this from the corner of the ceiling. I don't really remember anything else about that day.

CHAPTER 19

LITTLE BOY TRYING

There is this shroud through which I remember childhood.

Sometimes I can remember the most intimate details. To this day, whenever I pass a man wearing Mennen's After Shave the smell evokes strong memories. Once again, I become that little boy standing at the bathroom sink watching my daddy shave looking up at this huge man admiringly and wanting his love as I watch every detail.

He takes the razor and periodically washes the shaving cream off, and the whiskers wash down the drain. I can still feel his touch as he would put shaving cream on my chin and ask, "Is that a whisker I see there on your chin," as he shaved that one spot and we both would be grinning from ear to ear. He would take the towel and wipe his face and then wipe that one spot on my chin, and I would be filled with love and admiration as he wiped.

As I look back on those days, I think each time I watched him shave there was a part of me that wanted to crawl up into his arms and hide. Then, as a curtain dropping over a play, all of a sudden my memories cease; I can remember no more. The shroud cuts off a part of me that I cannot retrieve. No matter how hard I try, I cannot penetrate the shroud.

At some points, it becomes a veil and I catch partial glimpses of what must have been, but at other points, I am completely shut out. My memories of the fears of homelessness are surrounded by these shrouds and veils. There were multiple occasions during childhood when we were evicted or nearly evicted.

I sit outside the kitchen in the dining room and listen to my parents' discussions of losing the house. These discussions scare me more than my parents fighting, and I am struck with terror at the thought of having no place to live.

I have seen families put out of their houses before, and my mama tells stories of people in the neighborhood who have been put out. I have images in my mind of our furniture sitting out on the street in the dead of winter, and I am sitting in the living room lounge chair outside in the street as the wind blows. I cannot get these images out of my mind, and each time our heat is cut off I worry about this eviction thing even more.

Sometimes it is so cold in the morning. I do not want to get out of my bed, where it is warm and I am draped in blankets and quilts. My mama forces me to get up to wash up for school. She has boiled water on the stove and she pours a bowl of hot water to wash up with, and I wash my body as fast as I can as I watch my breath in the cold of the house.

I think that I am breathing harder and harder because I am trying to move so fast as the cold chills every part of my body where I put water to. My sister, my brother, and I all huddle around the kitchen stove as we dress for school as the burners and oven all run full blast.

I am especially glad to go to school today, where it is warm and I can relax. As my siblings and I head out the door into the winter air, I am excited and cannot wait to get to school. I like school. I get attention at school. Whenever I do well on my homework or on a class assignment my teacher seems to notice and this makes me feel good.

After I hang my coat and hat in the coat closet, I come out in the classroom and stand by the radiator with my back to it. The heat feels good and I stand by it a long time trying to warm my bones. The nun tells me to sit down at my desk, but I do not want to move, so I pretend that I do not hear her and continue to warm my bones. After a few minutes, she notices that I have not moved and she is angry. She proceeds toward me hurriedly and screams at me at the top of her voice to go to my desk, and I am struck with terror.

This teacher can be very mean, and I do not want to get hit. I know that she wants what is best for me, but whenever I am struck, I feel like I am back at home in the midst of my parents' fights. Then I get nervous and scared, and I am struck with a terror that I cannot get out of so I spend the rest of the day in a dream world.

She does not strike me, though, but I do get detention for not paying attention. I don't care because I am not in any hurry to get back home. For most of the morning, no matter what I do, I cannot get warm enough.

I think that I am still nervous because I thought that the teacher was going to hit me. Once I get nervous like that, it is hard to get myself calmed down, but I try. Sometimes the harder I try the more nervous and anxious I become. I start worrying allover again. Are we going to lose the house and get evicted? It's so cold at home. Are my parents going to get angry at each other and fight again? If we get evicted, are they going to take my sister and brother away from me? My mind is racing and I cannot make it stop!

The nun has asked me a question and I have no idea what she is talking about. I have not been paying attention as she was writing on the blackboard. I suspect she knows I have not been paying attention, so I try to hide and hope she does not realize I am just not here today, but it is too late.

I get more detention for not paying attention. My mama's words race through my mind: "Michael, you're not put together too tight," or "Michael, you know that you're not all there."

I feel bad. I spend the rest of the day pretending to pay attention while staring at the blackboard. As I walk home from school that day I am afraid, because I know I am going to get in trouble for getting detention.

My mama asks, "Why did you get in trouble and what did you do?" I reply, "I don't know, I didn't do anything." My mama sends me to my room as I try to figure it out, but I cannot. As hard as I try, I cannot figure it out. I think that I am afraid that there might be something wrong with me, but I am even more afraid that I cannot figure out what it is.

I am hurt and disappointed; I have let my mama down, once again. As I think about this shroud and the veils through which I remember childhood sometimes, I am frustrated that sometimes I cannot remember more. I think to myself, "if I could only remember this" or "if I could remember that." Then once again, I become that little boy and as hard as I try, I cannot figure it out.

Then again, sometimes I suspect that the shroud and the veils may be my greatest source of strength. Maybe the shroud and the veils protect the little boy I cannot stand to be and whom I cannot protect and yet I am.

CHAPTER 20

GOD, PLEASE HELP, PLEASE HELP ME, PLEASE?

The first stories I ever heard of my own drinking were about how one of my uncles gave me beer when I was in my high chair. My parents and uncles used to tell the story and laugh about how I started acting funny and blowing bubbles with my own spit. I was always enthralled whenever I heard that story.

It made me feel as if I was a member of the family. I was like my uncles, the men I admired and wanted to be like, and I was like them from the earliest possible age. In a way, that story made me feel special. I think I felt that way because in childhood I always felt as if I was on the outside, looking in especially when it came to my family.

That story made me feel as if I was on the inside. My mama said she got angry with my uncle that day, but I could tell she also thought it was funny. As she would tell the story she would be amused just as much as anyone else in the family. Often she would even initiate the telling of the story. I think she enjoyed being seen as the protector of the family, especially when it came to that particular uncle, someone whom I always felt she did not particularly care for anyway.

Throughout the years, I would occasionally ask my father for a sip of beer. I don't really know why, at the time I certainly did not enjoy the taste. Maybe more important than enjoying the activity, I was extremely curious about the activities of the adults around me. I wanted to be like the rest of the family. I think that is why I always enjoyed the story of my uncle giving me beer in my high chair. It portrayed me as a member of the family.

Sometimes on Sundays when my family would be at my daddy's favorite brother's house, I can remember asking my father for a sip of beer. I would ask my daddy, and my cousin would ask his daddy. Both men would give us our sips, and we would laugh at my younger cousin because each time he had a sip he would hold his head back and say "aahhh" in an exaggerated tone.

He, my siblings, and I would then go off to play or continue to sit in the room watching the adults around us, but satisfied that our request was honored.

From time to time, my sister and other cousin would get in on the action, but I remember my youngest cousin more than I remember any other. Maybe because we were both eldest sons' although this cousin was an only son, but more importantly, we were family, doing what our family did.

I suspect my mama took pride in this, because she would comment that her children had no reason to be sneaking a drink or doing what other kids were doing in the streets. Sometimes she would follow up these comments with, "I'm growing up with my kids." As I look back on those days, ironic it seems that, as far back as I can remember, my siblings and I always did everything else in the streets that any other kids were doing.

After we moved out of my grandmother's house onto South Twelfth Street, my daddy had two different places where he would hide liquor. In the bushes directly in front of the house was one, but the other and more common place was the bushes in the backyard. It would always be a half pint or a pint of vodka. I always thought it was a pint or half pint because the bottles were easily hid in the growing hedges. For years before I ever took my first drink on my own, I would re-hide my daddy's liquor, especially whenever it was in the hedges in front of the house. I don't really know why I would re-hide it. I suspect I was ashamed of my daddy's drinking, and if I could find the bottle that easily, I figured that either the neighbors or my mother could find the bottle also. So I would take the bottle and bury it farther into the bushes, sort of like putting it away for safekeeping for my daddy. I can remember doing this while thinking of my grandfather, whom I had sat on the porch with in Georgia and watched drink vodka out of a water glass years before.

Once I remember watching my father from the back window as he went up and down the hedges looking for his liquor, and then I felt guilty because maybe I had hidden the bottle too well. He never did find the bottle that day. He came into the house and sat down at the kitchen table. My mama asked him, "What's wrong?" and he replied, "I need a drink," as she went into the next room about her business of folding the laundry.

I went outside to search for my father's bottle of liquor, but it was nowhere to be found. I figured he was drunk when he hid it or maybe he really didn't have the bottle of liquor in the first place, but I really didn't know.

As I look back on those days, I realize that I always saw my father as a weak man and a man who truly needed my help. More than that, I suspect, I always saw his vulnerability. However because I was a child, I was not sure of what I was seeing. This part of him made me love him even more. Ignorant of my own feelings at the time, I now suspect that the part of my daddy that made me love him was also a part of me that was still unattended to.

I had a similar feeling when it came to my sister, although not as strong. It always seemed that my sister bounced back and forth between anger and fear. It was as if she was trapped. Although my feelings were different at the time, rarely if ever experiencing anger, I felt this sort of familiarity and empathy for my sister. I think the part of her that I could identify with was the part that felt trapped. I knew that no one could ever get to this part of my sister, or at least no one had gotten to that part of her as far as I knew, but still I could feel that part and I knew that it was there. I feel it is the part that needed to be loved. I knew that I had that part within myself also, although I never would have admitted it at the time.

It was the first weekend after the terrorizing experience in the bathroom with my mama. My parents had a bottle of Manischewitz wine in the dining room buffet. I had never done this before, but I went into the cabinet and took a drink. I got a warm oozing feeling all the way down my body. It was wonderful and I loved it.

Later on, my friend Virgil and I went around the corner on Avon Avenue. We waited outside the liquor store and asked several people going inside to buy us liquor if we would give them the money. Several said no, until one man said yes, provided we bought his liquor also.

My friend and I spent the rest of the night walking up and down the streets in the neighborhood drinking our liquor. As I got drunker and drunker, I noticed that I felt better and better. No longer was I worried that my parents were going to kill each other. No longer was I worried that my parents we were going to lose the house. No longer was I afraid of my mother. No longer was I worried about the embarrassment of our neighbors seeing the police coming to our house on what seemed like every weekend. No longer was I worried about my mama beating up my sister or my daddy.

For the first time in my life since my grandmother had died, I felt wonderful! Now, I understood the amazement of the adults around me. Although I had tasted alcohol before, this was the first time in my life that I ever felt like that. More than anything else about that night, when I think back I remember being worry-free. I don't think that I knew how to be worry-free until that experience.

Later on, Virgil and I sat on the steps in front of my house and we drank one bottle after another. We told jokes and laughed and laughed as if everything, including the very air itself, was funny. Virgil eventually went home and I sat there by myself. As I sat there still experiencing this delightful event with a power I had never known, I started to feel sad. My parents, and sister and brother were away and I sat there on that porch alone.

I thought about my parents coming home, and all of a sudden I was afraid - not that they would catch me drinking, but that, they would come home and start fighting again. The police would come and, once again, my daddy would be off to jail. Somehow, some way the violence destroyed this wonderful feeling that I had experienced. My feelings of delight changed from joy, wonder, and amazement to fear, terror, and depression. I did not want the joy to end.

I wanted to feel good forever, but I could not stop my mind from racing. My sadness turned into tears and then into rage. I hated my father and my mother. No matter what I do, it seems like I cannot get away from them. Their violence destroys me. I cannot stop thinking about it. I am coming apart and crying violently. I am afraid and of what I know not. I am transported once again to that boy in the tub in terror.

I feel the same way I do right before I am getting ready to crash into a wall. I cannot help myself this time, and I want to die. I just want to die. As I walked up the steps into the house, I could not think of anything else but I want to die. I walked through the dining room, kitchen and into the bath. My mind is running away from me. I stare at my arms longingly, looking for the welts that usually lined my arms. I cannot find the welts tonight. I feel they are there and oozing with blood once again. As I fill the bathtub with water, I am in the drain, the corner of the ceiling, and a hundred other places I have been a thousand times before.

I pray the same prayer I had prayed my entire childhood it seems like a thousand times before. "God, please help me, please help me, please," but God just doesn't seem to care.

My next memories are of my mama dragging me from the bathtub soaking wet, still dressed. From what I can remember, apparently I had been unconscious. My parents laughed about that episode for years. My mama would say, "I've never seen anyone take a bath fully dressed before in my life," and she and my daddy would chuckle.

For the remainder of my childhood I always felt stupid whenever I heard that story. My mama would look at me and say, "I keep telling you you're not screwed on too tight," as I would shriek with this horrible pain from within.

CHAPTER 21

LEARNING ABOUT EARNING

By the time I was thirteen I would from time to time try to earn some money. I do well whenever it snows. My siblings, several of our friends and I go throughout the entire neighborhood. We charge people to dig out their cars, driveways, or sidewalks. We start early in the morning and stay out all day until dark. Sometimes it snows two or three days in a row, and we go back to the same people all over again. I can remember having well over twenty or thirty dollars on many occasions and that much money lasts for quite a while.

Sometimes I buy myself a new pair of dungarees or a pair of gloves or add to my baseball-card or comic-book collection. At other times, I put it in my piggy bank until I can decide what to do with it.

It is during this time that my daddy first starts borrowing money from me. He has to go to work early in the mornings because he has to be to work by six. I am sleeping in the top of my bunk bed and he shakes my legs around five in the morning when it is still dark. "Hey,

Slim, Slim, you woke?" I wake up, and he says, "Do you have fifty cents I can borrow?" This happens every Monday.

Sometimes it happens on other days, but it happens every Monday. He needs bus fare to get to work so he can borrow money from his boss. Often I give him two or three dollars because I feel sorry for him. I love my daddy a lot and I want to do whatever I can for him. He usually pays me back on Friday when he gets paid, but sometimes he does not come home over the weekend and he forgets to pay me back, but I really don't mind.

My mama tells him not to borrow money from the kids, but he does it anyway and they sometimes laugh about it under their breath. Sometimes I think he is embarrassed to ask, so he sneaks into my room and goes into the pocket of my dungarees and takes what he needs. I pretend to be asleep, but I watch him out the corner of my eye. Sometimes he'll shake me and say, "Hey, Slim, I got some money."

Often he says nothing. Sometimes I have things I want to do with my money, so I take my wallet out of my pants when I go to sleep and I put it on the inside of my pillowcase. When I go to bed early enough and I can remember, I take my wallet and hide it outside in the bushes but I always take a couple of dollars inside to give to him. This way I can always make sure I have enough for me. He's smart though, and sometimes when I hide my money, I can hear him taking money out of my piggy bank. When I don't have any money, he'll wake up my brother who sleeps just below me in our bunk bed, but I usually try to keep some money, especially for Mondays.

The first time I went to get a social security card, they would not give me one. I was not old enough, but as soon as I had a birthday I went back to get myself one of those cards so that I could get a job.

I didn't get my first real job until I was fifteen and I planned every week for what I would give to my daddy. He knew that he could depend on me, and that made me feel good. I think that my mama always wanted me to get a job. She is always talking about this friend that she works with who has four sons and all of them work. I think she is very impressed by this so I planned on getting a job as soon as I could. Her friend even has one son who bought a car.

There is a part of me that really doesn't want to get a job. But somehow, I feel that I have to; it is the right thing to do. My mama is struggling hard to feed and clothe us, and she talks about how much my daddy drinks up his paycheck all the time. I still eat a lot, probably more than I used to. I quit the track team at school so I could work.

I love running track. Two or three times a week, my coach sends us on these long six-to ten-mile runs. The first mile is always the hardest. He sends the entire team. We all start out together. I have learned to pace myself though. Some of the guys start out fast, but I just start out trying to make myself comfortable.

I know that I will pass them up before it is all over with. Something happens to me during these runs. I like it a lot when I get to about the third or fourth mile. It is as if my body just starts to work on its own and I glide over the miles. I always like the sixth to eighth mile best, and when we time ourselves these are always my fastest miles. I start to feel good and I forget about everything that is worrying me. Every now and then, I'll think back to home and my parents or the fighting, or how we never seem to have enough money, but somehow when I am running, these thoughts never seem to stay with me long. It is as if whenever I am running I just don't seem to be able to worry for long. I enjoy the feel of my body, the air passing back and forth through my lungs, and I can even sense when the wind changes direction. I like to feel the sunshine on my skin, and I admire the grass, trees, and streams that run through the park. I am one of the few guys on the team that enjoys these long runs. My coach thinks that I am a hard worker, but really, it is just that I somehow lose myself on these long runs and it feels good. I do not tell him otherwise, though. After the run is over, I continue to feel good for quite some time.

If my parents fight on a night after one of these long runs, it doesn't seem to bother me as much. I am even able to sleep on these nights all the way through the night.

I run cross-country and, during the indoor season, I run the 880. I started out as a miler, though, but I am a better half-miler. My school has four teams, freshman, sophomore, junior varsity, and varsity. I run on the junior varsity team my sophomore year. I also run on the sophomore and junior varsity two-mile relay team. I really like that. I remember the day I quit the team. It was the first week of my junior year in high school. I told my coach that I had to quit, that I wanted to work because my family needed the money. I think he was disappointed. He told me that I would probably be running varsity, but I quit anyway.

I lied to my track coach that day. I really didn't want to work. As I walked away from him, I could feel his eyes on my back, and I was hoping that he was going to call me back. I wanted him to tell me that I could run and that I really didn't have to work. I think that I wanted him to tell me that I could do whatever I wanted to do, that I really didn't have to worry about my parents. I think that I wanted, and maybe needed, him to make sense of my life.

In a way, I think that I am a little bit afraid to run track. It's like no matter how hard I try, it is never quite good enough. I do rather well and have accumulated quite a collection of medals from various meets I have run in, but somehow I am never satisfied. It is this eerie feeling on the inside. Maybe what I really wanted from my track coach that day was for him to tell me that it was O.K., that I was O.K., that no one was going to hurt me and that everything was going to be O.K. I remember one day my coach entered me into a quarter-mile race. I am not even a quarter-miler, but I guess he needed me to run the quarter that day.

It is a very large field in the race and I am not the only one from my school in the event. The gun goes off and I start out, comfortable to settle back in the middle of the pack as we round the first turn.

I am still a little bit nervous still from the fight my parents had last night. As we come out of the turn, suddenly I see a freshman from my school pass me on the outside. I am shocked and appalled - the nerve, I am a sophomore and apparently he doesn't know that. All of a sudden, I am determined that I am not going to be embarrassed by this snot-nose, wet behind the ears freshman who obviously doesn't know his place. All of a sudden, I move to the outside. Before I know it, I have run past the freshman and the entire field and I am rounding the last turn and running as hard as I can without regard to anything. I am determined I might collapse at the finish line, but I don't care, I am definitely going to wax this snot-nose freshman and the rest of the field.

As I slowed down after crossing the finish line, I felt this sense of exhilaration and excitement. I didn't win the race that day, but I did come in third and I got a bronze medal. More importantly, I left that snot-nose freshman in the dust.

Although I don't win the race, I do win something. I am not real sure what it is or even why it is so important. I have always remembered that day and that feeling of excitement and exhilaration as I crossed the finish line. I don't think that was the greatest effort I made throughout childhood but I think it was important because it is the only effort I ever made without fear.

Maybe what I really wanted from my track coach that day I quit the track team was a chance. A chance to try something that I really wanted and a chance to try it without fear. Maybe I just wanted that feeling of supreme exhilaration and excitement once again.

I think I needed and wanted a "playground," a place to experiment with and in. I needed a place to test my limits during childhood. I needed a place to find out who I really was and what I really was without having to worry about whether my parents were getting ready to kill each other.

I needed to know what it felt like to try my best at something that I and only I wanted without fear. I think I needed permission to have that feeling. When I think back to those days, I often wonder how good I could have been, but, I accept that was not to be my story.

I started working in a chemical research laboratory. I mop the floors and clean the toilets.

All of the people who work there are chemists, and they do some type research on plastic resins. Sometimes I melt down their plastic resins for them, but this job is very hot and I wear an asbestos apron and gloves. I wear this see-through face mask to protect my eyes and face from the heat.

I have to stand in front of this red-hot press to do this job. I don't mind mopping the floors or cleaning the toilets, but whenever I have to melt the resins, I get soaking wet from the heat and sweat. All of the chemists treat me really well, and it is very nice being able to have my own money.

I start buying my own books and my own clothes and I pay my own bus fare back and forth to school. I no longer have to ask my parents for much and I like that, but I really wish my daddy would stop taking my money. But I don't think about it much. I am his son and I know he has the right.

Sometimes I forget to put my wallet in my pillowcase, but it is O.K. Even when he asks me, I never say no. Sometimes I give my mama money on payday and I think she likes that a lot. I buy my own lunch too.

I work a lot of hours, as much as I can because I don't want to ask anyone for anything. They even let me work on Saturdays sometimes, and I like that a lot. Although I am just a teenager and still in school, I feel rather grownup. I think my mama was right, "there is nothing like having your own." I play in the concert and marching band at school. Then I go to work. I am president of my class and I am president of the black students' organization.

I am so tired by the time I get off from work and it is dark and then I have to go home and do my homework. I take the bus home. The bus ride is long. Sometimes I fall asleep on the bus and when I wake up, I am at the end of the line in Irvington. Then I have to ride the bus back down to Newark to get home. When I get home, I do my homework then I go to sleep. I do this every day.

Sometimes I fall asleep while I am doing my homework, but I like doing homework. I lie down on the living room floor and spread my books out in front of me and go to it. My parents are good when I am doing my homework and they never, ever bother me when I am. They even make my sister or brother leave me alone when I am doing homework. I think I like doing my homework because I like the peace and quiet and I like being left alone.

My parents usually fight on the weekends, so I can sometimes get a lot done between Monday and Thursday. Sometimes I read ahead in books a few chapters. I always try to stay ahead of the class. That way when my parents start fighting and I don't have the time to study, or when I just get too worried, anxious, or upset to study, I can still get good grades. My parents like it a lot that I continue to get good grades, but sometimes it is very difficult.

I stood up in class one day to answer a question for my teacher and I fainted. They took me to the doctor, but he says that I am not sick, just exhausted. I spend a couple of days in bed before I go back to work and school, but my parents are very proud of me.

CHAPTER 22

CHILDHOOD'S FONDEST FANTASIES

I don't remember being held, hugged, or coddled by either of my parents' during childhood, but there were times that almost made up for that lack of affection.

I could not have been more than three or four years old at the time, but I can remember the sheer ecstasy of riding atop my daddy's shoulders my legs wrapped around his neck and holding onto the top of his head as tight as I could as I sensed the up and down of his every step. I would sway forward with every step, and as he took the next I would sway backward as I grasped on tighter, sometimes my hands sliding over his eyes as he would shout, "Hold on, Michael, I gotta see," and he would gently reach up and nudge my hands away from his eyes. I would be grinning from ear to ear. I would be laughing and loved riding atop my daddy's shoulders.

I could see the whole world from there. My baby brother wrapped in his blanket is riding in my mother's arms and my baby sister is running back and forth all over the store and from here I can see us all.

As I recall those days I wonder how my parents got any shopping done with three small children hanging onto their every move, but I really didn't care, I just wanted to be with them. I like watching my sister, especially from this angle. She is so happy and in every aisle she spots something and runs up to my mama with, "Mommy, mommy, can I haff tis?" Sometimes my mama says no and sometimes my mama says yes, and sometimes I think that my mama is as tickled with my sister as I am as I watch us all.

There have been many times since those days when even as an adult I have walked through a grocery store and longed to be atop my daddy's shoulders one more time while watching my family. It strikes me as odd that, although I grew up to be bigger and taller than my father, there is still some part of me that is still small within my heart and would trade everything just to be atop his shoulders one more time and to experience that wonderful feeling of joy. I think that my father knew that I enjoyed riding atop his shoulders, and for each ride that he gave, I am grateful a thousand times over.

While we were still in my grandmother's house, my father would sometimes sleep on the living room floor. I can still hear him snoring as my siblings and I would crawl over him and jump up and down on his chest and stomach until he finally woke up. Sometimes he would briefly wake up and tickle each of us, but more often than not he simply laid there as the three of us explored, and searched inside his pockets, his ears, his nose, and eye sockets, totally amazed at what we would find. I would take my hands and pry open his mouth and the three of us would search this voluminous cavern. I remember being amazed at the size of his teeth, almost as much as at the size of his feet.

I remember the three of us tiring and I would lay my head in his armpit or on the side of his chest with my sister and brother on the other side as we would all just lie there going in and out of sleep. I think my family did this a lot after my grandmother died. I have memories of all five of us on my grandmother's bed taking our Sunday afternoon naps, my mother and father in the middle of my grandmother's bed with my siblings wrapped in each of their arms as I lay at the bottom hugging my daddy's feet. These were some of the most joyous times of my childhood and these, I will not forget.

Ironic as it may seem, I have always perceived childhood as a time of dreams, hopes, wants, and aspirations, but as I look back on that period of my life, it was hopes, dreams, wants, and aspirations I rarely had. Some part of me had become afraid to dream or to fantasize what I really wanted, and I don't know how or when this happened.

I was afraid to dream my fondest fantasies. I think that I depended upon my parents to make these fantasies come true or at least to help them on the way, and I had given up hope that they would ever be able to do this.

Unlike many of the things I write about here, which were unconscious at the time, I believe my inability to hope for my greatest fantasy was a conscious decision: that I just could not depend upon my parents for anything. What I hoped and dreamed about more than anything was that I could live in a home without fear or violence. This was my greatest fantasy! As a child, I spent many an hour down on my knees praying to a God who certainly was not listening, "God, please help me, God, please help me, please?" Although this was my greatest fantasy of childhood, except when I was praying I spent little if any time pondering what it would be like to live in such a home. It was almost as if I was unable to imagine such a place. It was beyond my ability to imagine.

I remember the day I decided that I could not depend upon my parents. It was soon after my grandmother had died. The whole family was in Bamberger's department store and my baby brother asked my father for a winter coat. My father looked at him and replied, "Why do you need a coat?" My brother became angry and told him, "To keep my ass warm, why in the hell do you think?" My brother could not have been more than seven or eight years old at the time. Then my parents got into an argument right there in the middle of the store.

I made the decision at that moment in my life that I could not depend upon these people, and I have never regretted that decision, nor have I ever changed my mind. Some part of me wished that my father would stop drinking, but even this was never on a conscious level. It was more a reflection of all the long discussions which my mama and I used to have, and I thought that it was a way to make her happy. Which brings me to my other fantasy, that my mama would love me? This fantasy hurt the most! I can still remember the day I decided she would never love me. I was playing Little League baseball. It was a day I had struck out three times.

I came home sad and depressed. I was standing there in the kitchen feeling very low as my mama glared at me and asked, "What's wrong with you?" As I replied, "I don't know, I just feel sad;" she caught me with a left fist to the mouth. For whatever reason, this is the blow that I remember most throughout childhood and the one that I reflect back to most often.

The anger built up inside me as I tasted the blood from that blow. Maybe I think back to that occasion because there was a part of me that felt attacked and wrongly so. I had done no wrong and committed no act other than to answer the question that had been posed. As she glared into my eyes that day, once again racing back past everything I had ever learned to do to protect myself, I felt a feeling that I had never felt before. I felt hatred. In that moment, I hated her as much as I could, and for the only time in my childhood, I stared back at her, straight into her eyes. I was not thinking anything, I was feeling hatred.

Much to my surprise, she only struck me one time that day, but I believe our relationship changed that day and I no longer sought her love.

It was simply too much to hope for; however I did continue to seek her approval. That day was the only time throughout childhood that our eyes met fully engaged in combat.

If I could have had a fantasy during my childhood, my ability to stare my mother back would have been one. I don't know why this was important, however a part of me was trained that this was the deadliest of all sins. My ability to restrain my most primitive instinctual drives was paramount to my ability to survive in that home.

Now that I look back on that situation and realize that, as I was being attacked, my need, my want, and my right to strike back was not only real but also a most appropriate human emotion. There is a mourning that I feel as I think of the loss of my innate instincts to protect myself from harm and of all of the situations later when I have been unable to fend for myself because of this learned trait.

Most of the things that were in the forefront of my mind during childhood had absolutely nothing to do with me: the violence, the drinking, the need of my parents' love and approval. So, it has been difficult since to shed light on my own instinctual needs, wants, and desires, never mind my fondest fantasies and the thought of working to make these fantasies come true. This was beyond my ability to perceive.

If I could get back anything from childhood, I would want to get back the fantasies, not the logical, seemingly possible ones, but the wild, wistful ones the whimsical ones that sparked my imagination and lit my dreams. The ones which my parents convinced me were dumb and stupid. These are the dreams I miss the most, along with that part of myself that was within.

I feel the sadness, but not the pain that somehow was part of their destruction. It is not so much the specifics of this loss as it is that I had lost my ability to dream and, maybe more importantly, how to act in my own best interests in order to make dreams come true.

My mama stares at me with an all-consuming look of contempt, rage, and suspicion and calls me stupid, dumb, and a jackass once again. I am scared and I do not know what to do. I can hardly remember this episode simply because there were so many and it happened because of my hopes and dreams to be a good baseball player maybe even a major-league baseball player. My sadness the day I struck out three times was over my desperation to be a good baseball player.

The blow I received as I revealed this to my mama I have thought about for years. I am unsure if the blow was for striking out or if the blow was for being sad. I cannot figure it out.

Sometimes I am sad and about more than just baseball, but I never reveal this sadness to my mama. There is something scary about telling my mama about my sadness and I am scared to death to do so. This is not the first time I have been struck for being sad. Whenever I am sad, I go to my room to be by myself, or if my brother is in the room I go for a walk. I walk a lot.

I know that I am not to be sad, but sometimes I am overwhelmed and I cannot help myself. I try to figure out what is wrong with me and I cannot. The more I think about it the worse it becomes. Sometimes I think that I am crazy and my mind races and I cannot get it to stop.

I think that my mama despises me, hates me, and no matter what I do, I cannot get her to love me. I think she hates the person I am weak, confused, and, as she says, "not put together too tight." I try to become the person that she wants me to be, but somehow I never quite get to where she wants me to be.

Sometimes I hate her for this. I want to strike her back so she can feel the blood in her mouth and feel my knuckles against her head the way I have so often felt hers. I hate her and I love her. There is no one who hurts me or causes me more pain. It is almost as if she doesn't even know when she is hurting me and sometimes, as she is yelling and screaming at me at the top of her lungs and calling me dumb, stupid, and jackass, I just want to cry out at the top of my lungs: "Mama, stop, mama, stop, mama, stop, you're hurting me."

Yet I am unable to utter a single word as she tears, rips, and shreds my heart into pieces that I am unable to put back together again.

I suspect that my hopes, my dreams, and my fondest fantasies are still lying there on the floor of that house on South Twelfth Street in Newark, New Jersey, along with the pieces of my heart that I am no longer able to gain access to. I cannot describe this destruction, it is beyond my ability to comprehend, but I know that it was complete.

It was not my mother who destroyed these fantasies, it was I. How ironic. The child I once was who was ruthless in his efforts to destroy anything and all things that were to interfere with being other than what my mother desired. I now feel isolated, trapped, and abandoned due to my own destruction and ruthlessness for the totality of the destruction is beyond repair and I am unable to put things back together again.

Thus, I now feel the contempt for myself that I once felt from my mother. I cannot grasp my own anger and rage, for they were a part of the destruction, and I long for their repair.

CHAPTER 23

CHILDHOOD'S GREATEST FEARS

I was afraid my entire childhood. It was as if I lived in a well of fear and I was unable to see to the top I was trapped at the bottom. My parents, who controlled the bucket that could pull me out of the well, were either unwilling or unable to pull me out; regardless the result was the same. I was trapped!

I could handle some of the fears. Fear that my daddy would not come home with his paycheck and we would be hungry. Fear that my parents would be unable to pay the mortgage and we would be homeless. Fear that my mama was going to beat me senseless. Fear that my mama was going to kill one of us with that butcher knife. I had developed ways to handle all of these things at least as best I could.

However, there was always an underlying current of fear within me. This fear I always had difficulty grasping, holding onto, and reasoning with. For lack of a better way to describe it, it was simply a fear of the unknown, and there were many unknowns within childhood. It was like the undertow in a river. When you look at the surface of the water, you sense the power of the unseen force underneath you respect its strength, maybe stand in complete awe of it. If this undertow is a metaphor for what I was feeling at the time, it had the same physical properties; for I knew that it was something to be avoided definitely not to go swimming in lest I be pulled underneath never to be found again. If this river were ever to reveal my body again, it would spit me up miles from where I had been drawn in, but drowned just the same.

Somehow, I knew this as a child, I instinctively knew this. Thus, my only defense from drowning was to avoid being consumed in this river of feelings and emotions. My emotional, mental, spiritual, and ultimate survival was totally dependent upon my ability to avoid the tough undertow of this emotional river. This was a valuable characteristic to develop for the survival of my childhood.

What was completely necessary to survive childhood for so long is sometimes completely useless for my adult life, for there are times when it is necessary to cross an emotional river in order to get to the other side. If one has spent a lifetime avoiding the river, then it is difficult learning the necessary skills of swimming. Moreover is terrorizing the thought of entering the water.

This same water that in my mind kills. This same water that I have spent a lifetime trying to figure out ways to avoid. Here I believe lies the single most necessary challenge to overcome from surviving a childhood such as my own. When I think about those times of overwhelming fear I ask; What was I afraid of? It hurts to admit that I was most afraid of losing my parent's love.

I wanted and needed their love. I was completely dependent on their love, not only for nurturing and guidance, but for food, shelter, and survival and the thought of the withdrawal of their love was more than I could bear. My parents were my first deities.

I did anything and everything to ensure that the love of my deities would remain constant, strong, and available. Yet, as I remember it, it was this love that was the most tenuous of all the necessities needed for childhood. It was this love that was always dependent upon my ability to be good, to get good grades, to make my parents proud, to be outstanding in everything I did, and it was this love that made me the most neurotic, worried me the most, and scared me beyond my ability to fully realize.

The challenges of childhood were not the challenges of life. They were the challenges to maintain my parent's love and thus to guarantee my survival. This is why I was always so nervous most of my childhood, because everything I did was based in this life and death struggle to survive. Nothing was ever simple and the thought of failure was not a recognizable option within the realm of my experience.

Inevitably, I never learned how to fail or how to recognize failure as a part of success. How to see failure as a growing and learning experience. How to learn from my mistakes and how to fail with dignity and grace. For me, every failure that I ever had was more a sense of proof positive that my parents were right, that I was dumb, that I was stupid, and that I was a jackass. Thus, each failure that I had fueled my apprehension of my right to exist.

The thought of being swept up in the undertow of that river was more than I was willing to risk and why not? For me, failure meant certain death, so I became unwilling to risk anything that I was not sure that I would not succeed in. Had I succeeded may have been just as bad as had I failed, for if I made it to the other side of the river, what was I to do? I would be standing there alone without parents or siblings to stand next to. No, it was safer standing on the side of the river that I was familiar with, though as miserable as it may be, at least I was familiar with it and had developed skills to withstand and tolerate, if not to prosper. More importantly, at least I would not be alone. I don't know if I could have survived the loss of my parents as a child.

I think this is why, even though there were times when I was extremely upset or angry with my parents, I never would voice my anger or confront my parents. So I turned my anger inward choosing to destroy myself rather than risk the destruction of those whose love I was so ultimately dependent upon.

If there is one thing I wish that I could have overcome in my childhood, I think this would be it: I wish that I could have overcome the constant fear of the loss of my parent's love, but the greatest tragedy of my childhood is that I could not think beyond it.

CHAPTER 24

CHILDHOOD'S GREATEST FAILURES AND SPIRITUAL PEACE

By the time, I entered high school I was convinced my mother hated me. I wasn't sure why, but in my heart of hearts I believed that she did. In my mind, it was not so much anything I had done, it was more a sense of who I was as a person. I questioned and often regretted that I existed. I was convinced that my existence caused my mother pain. There was no single act that persuaded me, but more a series of acts over a long period of time that had overwhelmed me, moving me to that point. There was this place in my heart that I felt only she could fulfill. I spent most of my childhood and adult life trying to fill that place and I never did. In my heart, there was a longing for her and eventually a mourning of her.

It was a hurt I could not rid myself of as hard as I tried. I have come to believe the answer is not in trying to rid myself of the pain or in trying to find the place within her that I long to lay my head upon if for no other reason than to rest. But the answer is in accepting and thereby learning how to live with the pain. I had to learn to accept the pain of the loss of mama.

Thus, I arrive back at this place that I lived in as a child standing there in disbelief, horror, and fear the same way I stood there so many times before, not believing what was occurring right before my eyes. I never would have admitted this as a child, but I have to admit it now because that place exists within me. I know it well. I can describe that place better and more accurately than I can describe any other. It was, and still sometimes is, a place of refuge.

As a child, it was a place of refuge because my parents were not in this place. While it may be a place of refuge, it also is a place of arid isolation. When I can find no other place, I will still retreat there where it is safe, warm, and quiet the same way I did as a child after my grandmother died, and I am grateful that that place, my place, and, for many years my only place, is still there.

There were many times that I spent all night lying awake in my bed trying to figure out what it was I had done wrong or what it was that my mother had expected me to be. When I thought that I had arrived at the answer, I tried and then tried again to be that person, but somehow, some way it was never enough.

I was lost in this incessant pool of confusion, horror, and disbelief that I could not get out of. Sometimes this place still pulls me continually, patiently, and sometimes inescapably into itself, but I no longer fight this place. Maybe it is because of this air of familiarity that establishes a feeling of comfort for me.

Somehow and sometimes, this place feels like home. It has always felt like home and maybe always will, but I realize there is no longer a need to run away from this reality. It is my place and in the strongest sense of the word, it belongs to me. It is quite all right, for it is who I am and may well be a part of whom I shall become.

There were, and sometimes still are times that I question my sanity, but my sanity is, like every other feeling I have ever had, fleeting, not something to hold onto, but more a thing to let go of, for within the letting go, there is also peace, serenity, and the essence of my soul.

Although I have not seen my father or mother for several years I realize that nothing has changed since those days when I was a child. I still do not know how to earn their love or, more importantly, their respect! I do not even know why it was important but I accept that it was.

My love for my father was more passionate than my love for my mother. In my heart, I felt as if my father needed my love more. Ironic as it may be, my father never said or did anything to request my love. He just seemed to need it more. He was helpless most of the time.

While my mother demanded my love continually pointing out all she did for my siblings and me often on a daily basis. Her rationale was sound, but, for whatever reason, it never served to make me love her the way she wanted to be loved, cherished, nurtured, and admired, although I did develop guilt over my inability to give her what she wanted.

As a child, I felt my father to be vulnerable, while I could not see vulnerability in my mother; therefore I sought my father's love, but only in the indirect ways of a child long after I had given up any hope of my mother ever loving me. This was true if for no other reason than I was never quite as afraid of my father as I was my mother.

Looking back on those days, I think that I wanted my father to care for me. I hoped and hoped again that he would come to rescue me and make sense out of this life that in essence was driving me crazy, but this was not to be in my childhood.

During childhood, there were times that I was angry with my father or frustrated with him and often disgusted with him, but I was never quite as afraid of him as I was my mother. He simply did not present me with the same degree of terror. I suspect this was the main reason I loved him so.

I could withstand the violence, the beatings, and the arguments that I witnessed and was a part of as a child. Horrible as they may have been, I had developed ways to survive, withstand, and tolerate that terrible sense of ambiguity that I lived with as a child.

What I could not withstand and what I believe to this day threatened the survival of my soul was that terrible sense of dispossession. That sense that my life, my soul, my essence, and my survival belonged, not to me, but to someone else. There was a sense of futile hostility that I was unable to stop. That sense that, as my mama stared into my eyes and raced back pass everything I had ever learned to do to protect myself, at some point I would cease to exist. To this, I was totally defenseless and feared more than any other act.

I get this sense of vulnerability and heightened sensitivity whenever I think back to those moments.

I believe that I was not afraid to die. I did too many things that at the time I questioned whether I would come out alive. Defending my sister as my mother was attempting to push her out of that second-story window was one and the one I think back to most often.

But I was afraid of living, for I did not know how to live, for no one had taught me other than what I had seen demonstrated before me. At the time when I needed to be learning how to live, I was in the midst of a monumental struggle for survival. Survival left little energy for learning anything not immediately necessary. This way of growing up yielded consequences.

I think that many of the fights I had with my mama were over this one point: that I was afraid of living without any sense of who I was, what I was, or what and whom I was to become. It was as if my sense of purpose and being itself belonged to her and not to me, and for this I was willing to fight, to struggle, and ultimately to survive. It was this that kept me going, protected me, and developed a sense of creativity that never left me.

The day my parents discovered me unconscious in the bathtub I know that I did not want to live. However, I now know that my sense of dispossession was so great that I felt as if my soul had left me. This sense of void and emptiness in my soul made life not worth living. That sense of void, awkward emptiness that I had felt so many times had grown in power and strength. While I could remember the feeling dating back to the best Christmas of childhood, its power had become overwhelming.

The feelings now were more powerful than I and I believe because of my fears I allowed them to grow and gain power. I do not say that as self-criticism, for when a child I acted as a child, but it is merely an observation. It is as if that part of me that was strong, confidant, and good, or the best part of myself was not in a place to thrive or flourish, so I simply fought to survive hoping and praying for another reality from which to be nurtured.

I was unable to think beyond my childhood reality and therein lay a tragedy; this is the essence of childhood. Ironic as it may sometimes be, that feeling of void, awkward emptiness was strongest when my mother and I were the closest.

Throughout childhood, I have no doubt that I was her favorite. As I have said, she talked with me longer and more passionately than with any other. It was at these closest of mother and son times I would feel the most dispossessed.

There were times that I felt hated by this woman I feared, but there were also times when I felt loved, however there was always a sense of awkwardness devoid of comfort about this love. The intensity and passion of her love were like the intensity and passion of her hatred and I was unable to handle either.

I wanted my father to rescue me. It was this intensity of emotion I wanted to be rescued from the most.

I loved sitting up talking to my mama into the wee hours of the morning, however I suspect there is some part of me that wished that it would have been my father sitting there. He would have talked to her as I spied and peered in on them from around a corner, as a child observing the adult world that I was confused about.

That nervous feeling in the pit of my stomach was closely attuned to the violence of my home. I was never quite able to rid myself of the feeling. I carried it around with me no matter where I went and it was my closest companion and it was this feeling most likely to bring me to tears.

As I think back to the days of my childhood, it is these two feelings of void, awkward emptiness and nervous, scared pain in the pit of my stomach that were the predominant feelings of childhood. These feelings were my closest friends and became the feelings I was most familiar and comfortable with. If our childhood home is a collection of the feelings and remembrances we had, then this was my home.

I knew neither of my parents well, but I suspect I knew my father better than I knew my mother. I only say that because there was always this sense of sadness deep within my father that I could always sense, and that sadness was within my soul.

I think it peculiar the little things in him that I took as a sense of solace in myself. I would sit there and watch him at the dining room table listening to his favorite blues artists: Bobby "Blue" Bland, B.B. King, Jimmy Smith. It was as if there was this part of his self that he was searching for and somehow this made me feel better as a child. It was as if I were not alone.

Not all of my childhood was sad. There were moments I shall forever remember as being happy, joyous, and free. However the violence, the loneliness, the abandonment, and the neglect seemed to penetrate its way into my every word, thought, action, and deed.

There are times that I remember being in sheer ecstasy. Our family's first trips to the Apollo Theatre, our rides on the Circus Lines ferry up the Hudson River, the first time I ever beat my daddy in a foot race or the first time I ever heard my mama brag about my report card. It is just that these times are forever tainted with times that I wish I could forget. I want to forget my daddy's blood splattering onto my face and into my mouth when my mother stabbed him. I want to forget washing my father's blood up off the floor. I want to forget watching my mother try to push my sister out of a second-story window. I want to forget feeling the terror of my mama beating me up as I stopped her from pushing my sister out of that window. I want to forget watching my mother attacking my father with a butcher knife or listening to the insults my mother hurled at my brother because she did not approve of his weight, and I want to forget watching my father being hauled off in a police car. These things I want to forget and forget forever, but as hard as I try, I cannot. They creep into my consciousness without warning.

As I think back to those days, I do not know which memories are for real. Was my childhood so terrible and awful that I do not remember it as it actually was, or was my childhood really a dream of cotton candy, wonder, and amazement and I seek to make it worse than it was.

My mother once said something to me I remember. She said, "I did the best that I could." I don't know why I remember that statement but I do, that statement brings up more questions than answers for me, though. How did I come to witness so many acts of violence? How was it that the police came to our house so many times, and especially how did I get cut by my own mama while she was fighting my father? The most important questions, though, are how did I never feel loved? How was I always so scared? How was I so confused and so alone?

Maybe these questions were not meant to be answered. Maybe these are simply the questions of an irate child who, as she often said, "wasn't wrapped too tight." All I know is that there is certainly insanity wrapped up somewhere, somehow within those questions, so I never ask them. I simply leave them alone. I make no judgment as to whether my mama did the best that she could. She says that she did, and I accept that she did. It was and is what is was and is. However, there are times that I think to myself, "Your best wasn't good enough," but these times are rare.

The statement "I did the best that I could" adds to my sense of insanity, not only about my childhood but about life. It explains nothing and I return to that point that I lived in as a child attempting to make sense of or discover a purpose out of that which has none. I cannot adequately describe the feelings I get when I hear that statement. It is as if I am wrong to question this life that was handed to me or to try to establish purpose and meaning in, and I take on these feelings of guilt, shame, and remorse for questioning powers greater than myself.

I am stuck, paralyzed, and trapped once again just as I was as a child, where my needs, wants, and aspirations are in conflict with my needs, wants, and aspirations. I need, want, and aspire to establish sense, meaning, and purpose to that which I involuntarily suffered through, but I also need, want, and aspire to obtain my mother's love, respect, admiration, and approval, and it becomes obvious that I shall never obtain those things by questioning what has occurred. Once again, I have become that confused child who for whatever reason I seek to grow out of.

It feels like my need for meaning, sense, and purpose of my own suffering ultimately will destroy my mother. My mother who gave me life, but without meaning, sense and purpose in this suffering I shall die, if not from insanity alone. This is my dilemma and there is no way out. My insanity unravels before me as an adult even as it did as a child.

Sometimes I react the same way I did as a child when I felt her hand wrapped around my arm as she sought to fling me into another wall, sink, or refrigerator. Just as a child when I thought to myself, she is so strong, so powerful and I screamed on the inside, "get your hands off of me," I return to those same feelings as an adult again, and I remain silent on the outside.

Just as a child when I knew that I was going to crash into a wall, sink, stove, or refrigerator and realized there was nothing I could do to protect myself, I am again defenseless.

This time it is not the wall, sink, or refrigerator, I shall crash into, but the wall is a wall of needs and wants for love, respect, and admiration. I have come to accept this is a need I can only minister to myself. That is why I no longer ask those questions of myself and/or especially my mother. It feels like being in my childhood kitchen. Once again, I am alone; however, I seek a power greater than myself to deliver me to a place more survivable than this place of suffering where I am familiar and perversely comfortable within.

About the same time that my mother made that statement to me, "I did the best that I could." I had the same conversation with my father.

I traveled to another state and spent days tracking him down the same way I did as a child when I would search through the Fifty Bar and the streets and alleyways trying to find him. As my father and I sat on the banks of the Cumberland River, I looked into his eyes and I asked, "When I was growing up, why was everything so crazy?"

"I was always confused, hurt and much of the time I felt like I was going crazy, in fact I thought that I was crazy and I still feel crazy most of the time."

As the tears started to roll down my face, I was ashamed. I don't know why, I just was. Maybe because I had not grown up to be the man that I thought I would be. I felt hurt, ashamed, and defeated probably more so than I ever had before.

My father became silent, his eyes welled up, and he stared at the ground the same way he had done years earlier when I was a child and we were standing outside his place of work together.

In a way, I had again become that child hoping that he would rescue me and make sense out of a life that seemed to have no sense, meaning, or purpose. He spoke gently and quietly as he said, "Michael, when you were a child I never cared about you, your mother, your sister, or your brother." All I ever cared about was where was my next drink coming from."

I asked, "Did you ever love me?" He looked at me fleetingly, never quite catching my eyes, and said, "No, I never loved you." Then he looked at me and said, "You know I really fucked up and I feel like I fucked you up and I want you to know that I'm sorry."

I don't know if it was what my father said that day or the way that he said it. He had this air of sadness, loss, and desperation when he said, "No, I really fucked up and I want you to know that I'm sorry." I don't know if I have ever loved my father as much during my life as I did in that moment.

Here was this man whose love I wanted more than life itself telling me that he never loved me and that he did not care about me and somehow I was falling in love with him all over again.

I stood up, grabbed his hand, and pulled him close to me and we just stood there for a moment holding onto each other. I held him while patting his back and said, "I love you," as he said, "Yeah, me too." Which was his way of saying he loved me. I wanted him to say I love you and I miss you, but somehow I knew that his "yeah, me too" was his way, and for the first time in my life I was realizing that in that moment he was loving me as much as he was capable of loving me.

It was not all that I wanted, but somehow it was enough. Then my father told me a story from his childhood. This was not one of those stories that he and my uncles used to tell when they were all together, but this was a story I had never heard before. This was a story that helped me see into my daddy's eyes and somehow into my own.

He said, "You know, when I was a child I ran away from home once. I couldn't have been more than eight or nine years old. Everyone was looking for me, but I was hiding underneath the crawl space of the house. I crouched there under that porch and I listened to my parents talk about what they were going to do when they found me. Then I got more and more scared and when they found me, my father made me search for a limb that was good enough to whip me."

"I had to find three or four limbs before he was satisfied and he gave me the worst whipping of my entire life. After it was all over with I had welts all over my entire body and they were dripping with blood." Then he asked me in a rhetorical kind of way, "Now why would you whip a child whose only sin was that he was afraid?"

We just sat there after that looking out into space, the same way we used to when I was a child and I would go to him for help. In that moment I realized my father was as confused as I.

You would think that a father telling a son that he never loved him or cared about him would hurt, but it did not. It was a relief!

I have never felt a greater sense of freedom or wholeness in my life than I did that day, in that moment, when my father told me he never loved me. He was confirming all my worst fears and suspicions. He was affirming what I always suspected and in a way had always known, but was afraid to believe.

I needed him that day to affirm that it was all right for me to believe reality. This denial of reality continually fed my childhood's anxious, neurotic feelings. As a child, I did not have the capacity to believe reality. I suspect the thought of believing what I was seeing was just too scary. I abandoned reality but what else can a child do?

I needed him to affirm my worst fears and suspicions. That day my daddy gave me my greatest sense of sanity, and, although I cannot explain it in words, for the first time in my relationship with my father, I felt connected to him. In that moment, we birthed authenticity in our relationship.

In childhood, my family was always so concerned with the way we thought things should be or the way we wanted things to be or the way we needed things to be that we rarely considered the way things actually were.

In that experience, my father was now explaining the craziness I felt as a child. All of a sudden, the violence, the void of caring that I felt, and all the things which I could never explain made sense. They all happened because he did not love or care about me. I could now stop the incessant questioning that I used to constantly berate myself with, because now I had an answer, but more importantly, I had an answer that finally made sense.

I suspect that none of the other answers I ever came up with made sense because to a degree each lacked the necessary ingredient of the authenticity of truth. I have never felt more sane or connected to another human being than I did the day my father told me he never loved or cared about me.

Many things my father did when I was a child were not good choices. He once took me and my siblings with him during the day when he was out of work to an X-rated movie that scared me to death and gave me nightmares. He once made my sister eat off the floor like a dog after he had slapped her so hard she flew backward and hit her head on the cabinet at the base of the sink. He said that if she was going to act like a dog, then he would treat her like a dog. He once ran over a lady with our car while he was backing up after picking my mother up from work and all of us were in the car, and he simply left the scene of the accident and left the woman there.

He rarely, if ever, showed any love toward his family. The only thing that I remember from childhood that he ever did that I interpreted he was doing because he loved his family was that he used to steal tablecloths from work. He worked at a textile factory and he would steal these tablecloths from the factory and sell them at the Fifty Bar, and sometimes he would take us out to eat with the money he made. However, the day he admitted to me he never loved or cared about me I think he made a good choice. I think his admission that he never loved me was a daring act of courage!

The consequences of that courage were I no longer had to define the experiences of my childhood as love. That finally allowed me to explore new definitions of love that led to new and better ways to live. I am still grateful!

I have not seen either of my parents in more years than I care to remember. My mother disowned me after the conversation where she told me that she did the best that she could. She broke all ties with me and got a message to me that I no longer existed and I would never hear from her again. At first, I was numb, then, I experienced anger that turned to rage, however over the years, I have grown to not feel anything. She rarely if ever crosses my mind any more. It just doesn't feel like it would be worth the effort. I suspect my heart had been broken by her so many times there were no more pieces left to break.

I am not sure which state my father lives in or even if he is alive. Sometimes the thought of searching for him fleetingly crosses my mind, but I never do. Maybe I realize that the search was always about giving him one more chance to love me, but I have grown to accept things as they are.

Maybe the search was about the fact that I loved him so intensely, I am unsure. Maybe the insanity of my childhood will forever tug at my soul, but the real gift is in realizing that my soul belongs neither to my mother or to my father, or to myself, for that matter, but to my God.

I continually failed in my struggle to earn my parent's love although I made a heroic effort. I saw my parent's as deities when I was a child. My relationship with my first deities sowed seeds of pain that bloomed throughout life. Because of that pain, I now know I cannot earn love. If God is love, then God cannot be earned, a gift is given. My childhood struggle to earn my parent's love was my attempt to control an environment and a situation that I did not have the power to even influence let alone control. The harder I tried the more I lost one of God's most valuable gifts, the gift of vulnerability.

My soul was never designed to tolerate the pain I suffered, especially as a child. While hope is hard to kill it is fragile within a child's heart. When I came to believe God would never answer my most burning prayer which was always, "God, please help me, please help me, please" my consciousness of my connection to God was ripped apart. At that point, I no longer had the power to sustain remaining within my reality; let alone my body. I had already disconnected from my first deities my parents' so disconnecting from a God who I had never seen, felt, heard and now did not believe would ever help me was actually easier to do. The seeds of my parental relationship bloomed within my divine relationship and each flowered pain in my life because I now am, was, and will forever be, unable to tolerate the pain of being disconnected from my creator. In re-establishing connection to my creator, I had to learn to do something that my entire childhood taught me to avoid. I had to learn vulnerability.

The violence of my childhood was a challenge but the physical wounds did heal. However, the violence affected my sense of not only self-worth but of self. This skewed sense of self along with the violence and coupled with neglect, abandonment, and verbal abuse imposed emotional, mental, and spiritual wounds that festered and became infected. It has been a life time clearing away the pus to allow for healing.

Telling this story delivers me from my suffering. I now realize the experience had little to do with me and more a result of the situation into which I was born. Maybe, just maybe, I can convert the pain into a gift through surrender?

If I were to be given a choice as to what parents' I would be born to in this world I would choose the parents I got. I have loved them as I have loved no other, and this shall remain eternal, for it is the song of not only my heart but of my soul. Still to this day, I long for their love, their heart, and their soul as reflected in their kindness, admiration, approval, and respect.

The things I have become that I most admire about myself have occurred not in spite of my parents but because of. My greatest gifts, my resourcefulness, my creativity, my imagination, and my resilience, are all a result of the parents to which I was born and the home in which I was reared.

So I imagine my soul standing there before God among a myriad of millions as God asks, "Who would like to go to earth and be the child of Alice Louise and Peter Jr.?" and there is a deafening silence in the audience.

God looks out and stares me straight into the eyes and asks, "What about you, Michael?" to which I cry out, "Oh yes, thank you."

My best friends in heaven, Yvonne and Peter, volunteered also. They knew we could do a better job together than we would separately and that we should be together on earth as we were in heaven. Thus, my first memory at the tender age of twenty-three months of anger, fear, confusion and resentment was not to come to pass until all three of us were together to face the job at hand.

THE END

ABOUT THE AUTHOR

Michael Williams was born in Newark, New Jersey and currently resides in Escondido, California. He has lived in the mid-south and mid-west. He is the eldest of three children and was raised in the greater Newark, New Jersey/ New York City metropolitan area. He attended the parochial school system for both grammar school and high school. While in high school he was required to read ten books each summer prior to the school year beginning. This experience along with listening to the stories of his father and half-dozen uncles during childhood was the dawn of his experiences with story-telling.

The genesis of his story is he could not remember his childhood and it was suggested he start a diary starting with his earliest memory as a way of incubating childhood memories. When he did the stories mounted and years later, that spiral note book became "Earning My Parents' Love." This is the first of a series of stories concerning the consequences of growing up in the midst of alcoholism, violence, and dysfunction and its redemption. The second edition of this work has only a few changes however the title is more true to purpose "Growing Up In Alcoholism, Violence & Dysfunction" and the Sub-title was the primary motivation when it was realized that the entire work was simply listening to the voice of the inner child that was always there.

SOON TO BE RELEASED

THE IDEA THAT MY PARENTS' DID THE BEST THAT THEY COULD PISSES ME OFF

Preface

Being pissed off is a necessity for forgiveness. For many of us, who grew up with alcoholism, violence or dysfunction there remains an unmet need for the reclamation and acceptance of our own {childhood} anger. Meeting the needs of the child we once were is a prerequisite to forgiveness.

For those of us who have the anger, we are offered suggestions, advice, prayers, books, classes, seminars, biblical references, slogans, spiritual guidance, exercises, chants and more as a resolution of childhood anger.

All of the above failed me. While well intentioned, they all skipped what for me, would become a necessary ingredient to the recipe. They failed to provide a hearing for my childhood voice. They would prove to be inadequate because they failed to affirm childhood feelings. Without an affirmation of my anger, I was unable to move beyond it because I had never really claimed or owned it in the first place {even or especially as an adult}. They were solutions without acknowledgement of the problem. Since no opportunity for voice or affirmation was available within childhood, no solution in adulthood would prove to be adequate unless the childhood voice within would be heard. This lack of voice within childhood is part and parcel of the perceived offense. This lack of affirmation was an unintended repeat of the childhood experience.

It is reasonable to expect any perceived repeat of the childhood experience would meet with resistance. My lack of tolerance for forgiveness was not a revolt against forgiveness it was a rebellion against the denial of my feelings; for the sake of forgiveness. I was unwilling to repress my childhood voice {again} and sacrifice the way that I really felt.

This is the story of why parental forgiveness often fails. Much of the counsel given is insufficient because it fails to consider "We Were Children".

For true forgiveness of parents to exist, there are prerequisites:
- There has to be a hearing {A sympathetic hearing from the child I once was}
- There has to be discovery {The pros & cons of the situation}
- There has to be a history {Evaluation of both parental and childhood patterns}
- There has to be an evaluation and an informed decision {By the adult child}

Without past childhood input, we have little idea of:
1. What we are forgiving
2. Why we are forgiving
3. Who we are forgiving

Without these ingredients, we lack the necessary road map of how to forgive.

Without childhood input, we have "shallow forgiveness" which lacks depth, meaning, and purpose. It lacks durable value because without the time, energy and effort of past childhood input the essence of the anger rarely gets resolved. Without childhood input, there exists a minimization of our own childhood.

Valuable things in life more often than not require work, including and especially parental forgiveness. Without close examination, it is never truly put to rest and like the Phoenix that is long lived and cyclically generated, the anger rises from the ashes; sometimes often, sometimes rarely but it does rise.

Many of the solutions which were offered did not require much work on my part and I gravitated to those. Most were recommendations of making a decision as to a way to feel and then imposing that decision upon my emotional reality. If I say that I should feel a certain way and I then verbally declare that I feel that way, then magically I do. For me the imposed verbal declaration became a form of emotional repression as opposed to growth because it provided little emotive resolution. It offered instant solution to an intricate challenge without analysis, evaluation, or consideration. These solutions lack depth, insight, and authenticity.

I gravitated to some because I was unable to tolerate the discomfort, the struggle, and the necessary effort to evolve a deeper and more lasting forgiveness. In short, I just didn't want to do the work. I didn't want to do the work because owning anger is uncomfortable, tedious, and disconcerting at best. This is my story of doing the work and as a result creating authenticity. The Phoenix of anger never rises from the ashes of authentic forgiveness because authenticity endures.